UNDERSTANDING DISABILITY

UNDERSTANDING DISABILITY

Inclusion, Access, Diversity, and Civil Rights

PAUL T. JAEGER

CYNTHIA ANN BOWMAN

Westport, Connecticut
London

Library of Congress Cataloging-in-Publication Data

Jaeger, Paul T., 1974–
  Understanding disability : inclusion, access, diversity, and
civil rights / Paul T. Jaeger and Cynthia Ann Bowman.
    p. cm.
  Includes bibliographical references.
  ISBN: 0-275-98226-2 (alk. paper)
  1. People with disabilities—United States. I. Bowman, Cynthia Ann,
1958– II. Title.
HV1553.J34 2005
305.9'08—dc22   2005013007

British Library Cataloguing in Publication Data is available.

Library of Congress Catalog Card Number: 2005013007
ISBN: 978–0–313–36178–4 (pbk.)

First published in 2005

Praeger Publishers, 88 Post Road West, Westport, CT 06881
An imprint of Greenwood Publishing Group, Inc.
www.praeger.com

Printed in the United States of America

The paper used in this book complies with the
Permanent Paper Standard issued by the National
Information Standards Organization (Z39.48-1984).

P

Contents

Acknowledgments

Disability is not exactly something you can put away when you are done writing about it, at least if you are a person who happens to have a disability. In some way or another, virtually every new day can provide unexpected experiences and subsequent insights into disability as a personal and social issue. Some of the most interesting and important realizations in this text, therefore, have resulted from interactions with strangers who caused some revelation through an action, attitude, or comment. Other insights come about from experiences not with other people, but with inanimate objects or places that offer some social expression of disability. So, in an odd way, anonymous strangers or actual things have affected much of the thinking behind this book. Common sense, however, dictates against thanking the telephone pole that I seem to perpetually walk into on my way to the library or the professor who once treated me to his theory on why a person with a disability should not be in law school because juries would never decide in favor of a client who could only afford to hire "a defective."

Fortunately, there are some specific people who deserve a great deal of thanks for helping bring this book into existence. Marie Ellen Larcada, our endlessly optimistic editor, has been an encouraging force in keeping this book moving forward. She deserves tremendous respect for putting up with the innumerable changes to the title and for eventually helping to create the final title. Cindy and I offer a heartfelt thank you, Marie Ellen.

I actually began to engage issues of disability as more than something I dealt with on a personal level when I was a teenager. In the ensuing years, many friends, colleagues, collaborators, and others have been kind enough to discuss many of the issues covered in this book, often willingly. Though many of these discussions in the past fifteen years have been of great importance, Gary Burnett, Kathleen Burnett, and Kim M. Thompson (all of the College of Information at Florida State University) deserve specific mention for helping me understand the true importance of the concept of access.

Two people were also kind enough to read this book as it coalesced to ensure that the material was intelligible to people beyond the world of disability studies. Carol M. Jaeger, a retired teacher and school administrator as well as my long-suffering mother, and Lesley A. Langa, a loyal friend and my favorite art historian, were both saintly enough to read through this text to provide a nondisabled eye (literally and figuratively) to the material and to make sure everything made sense.

This is the third book on issues of disability that Cindy and I have put together. Each book has come from our common background in education, a shared far-reaching interest in issues of disability, and similar personal experiences with disability. Disability is a personal experience. It is a social experience. It is a profound influence on an individual's life with both positive and negative aspects. For all of the personal and social ramifications of disability, however, the roles of disability in the lives of persons with disabilities are still insufficiently understood both by people with disabilities and by the rest of society. Cindy and I hope that this book will help readers better understand disability and its social implications. Understanding disability is vital to including persons with disabilities in society as equal participants.

Paul T. Jaeger

Introduction:
The Goals of This Book

Disability is an issue that touches the lives of a tremendous number of people. The world population of persons with disabilities has been estimated to include as many as 550 million, nearly twice the entire population of the United States. In the United States alone, 54 million people have a disability. Most people know someone with a disability, and many people have a family member who has a disability. The number of persons with disabilities continues to grow as the population ages in many parts of the world. If you live a long enough life, it is statistically likely that you will develop some kind of disability in your advanced years, as only 15 percent of persons with disabilities were actually born with a disability. Simply put, disability is ordinary. Yet disability is rarely considered as a societal issue in a thoughtful and humane manner.

Scholars often discuss it either as an abstract theoretical issue or as a medical problem. Disability does receive some attention in public and in the popular media, but frequently only when a major court case is occurring or, sadly, when a commentator expounds on the seemingly undue expenses of some aspect of social inclusion of persons with disabilities. The latter is seen most frequently in an outcry over the expenses associated with the education of a particular child with a disability, even though the expenses in such cases are usually far from typical. Primarily, though, issues of disability and persons with disabilities tend to be left to the social margins. In spite of such marginalization, however, disability is related to myriad interrelated social issues, assumptions, reactions, classifications, legal categorizations, and representations that fuel how persons with disabilities are perceived and treated.

People with disabilities face many barriers every day, from physical obstacles to systemic barriers to institutionalized prejudices. Often, the most difficult impediments to overcome are attitudes other people carry regarding people with disabilities. This backdrop of persistent inherent discrimination against individuals with disabilities in society creates considerable limitations on the amount of time that is devoted to a humane understanding of the issues related to those individuals. These social barriers also raise many questions about the role of persons with disabilities in society. Where are the voices of individuals with disabilities? Why have they been predominantly silenced? What led to this current status? Why does society classify and react to disability in the ways that it does? In a society that overtly welcomes and embraces diversity, why is disability often excluded in definitions of diversity in texts, professional organizations, and employment applications? How might the social roles of disability change? What might be the catalysts for such changes? As long as disability is marginalized from other facets of the human condition, it will not receive the necessary awareness and discussion. This book is meant to foster discussion of these questions and maybe provide a glimmer of an answer to each.

There is a consistent "otherness" in most discussions of disability. Disability is approached as a social problem or as a topic of research, from the third person, not as an interrelated set of everyday diversity, access, health, family, social, and economic issues. No historical or current society has committed itself to treating the physical, cognitive, and emotional differences in individuals with disabilities as a natural part of the human condition. However, persons with disabilities have been a part of every human culture that has ever existed. People with disabilities, no matter what their disability is, have shared experiences of struggle, of facing discrimination, and of learning to live somewhat differently than what has been deemed normal by other parts of society. These social forces, their origins, their effects, and how they must be reconsidered are the focus of this book.

Although this book is heavily researched and full of citations, the text is written so that any educated reader can understand it. This cross-disciplinary text is meant to provide an intellectual and thoughtful discussion of these issues that engages readers in a manner that is meaningful to scholars, students, and everyone else who is interested. It will have meaning to those readers who have a disability and to those who do not. The citations are meant to provide access points to delve deeper into specific areas discussed in this book. The brief vignettes woven throughout the pages of this text are meant to situate the issues in everyday life. Personal stories are a provocative and meaningful form of communication that can connect the reader in ways far beyond research and theoretical perspectives. As noted at the beginning of this introduction, disability as a social issue is important to every member of society. This book hopefully will provide new perspectives to consider for those who research issues of disability as well as a substantive framework for understanding disability as a social issue for readers who are just beginning to consider these topics.

This text engages a broad range of factors that shape the social standing, limitations, and rights of persons with disabilities. This book presents a unique combination of concepts that will hopefully serve to provide a more holistic picture of disability as a social entity. It addresses disability in contemporary society and the ways disability is socially classified. It examines the social reactions to disability, including historical attitudes toward disability. It portrays the daily lives of persons with disabilities as well as others' responses to those lives. It confronts stereotypes, prejudice, and misunderstanding. It discusses the representation of disability in a wide spectrum of media and explores the legal issues related to disability. By examining the reasons for the current social positions of disability, it will hopefully help to form a clearer picture of the range of issues related to disability in society.

All individuals with disabilities, as a result of the challenges that they face in society, are linked by the goals of being accepted and included by society and being treated with equality and dignity. For individuals with disabilities, true equality "incorporates the premise that all human beings—in spite of their differences—are entitled to be considered and respected as equals and have the right to participate in the social and economic life of society" (Rioux, 1994, pp. 85–86). The progress to true equality has been a very, very long one for persons with disabilities and it is far from complete. The reasons for this persistent inequality are explored in detail in this book.

The first part examines the social roles of disability through history to the present. Part 1 closely considers the various social classifications of disability, which primarily link the person to the medical condition. The social reactions to disability that result from these classifications, the history that led to these classifications, and the legal documents that encode and reinforce the classifications are discussed at length. Part I ends with an example, immigration policies of the U.S. government, where the confluence of social reactions, social classifications, and legal classifications of disability came together to create a situation of utter discrimination that affected not only persons with disabilities trying to immigrate to the United States, but also many other potential immigrants and persons with disabilities who were already U.S. residents.

Access and accessibility are the focus of part II. Access has been at the heart of disability rights as long as persons with disabilities have demanded equal treatment. Equal access to physical places, social systems, and intellectual content has been a central issue for persons with disabilities. The scope and meaning of access, physical and intellectual, are described as the basis of a discussion of the unique manners and issues of access for persons with disabilities. This part also explores the relationships between access and the legal classifications of disability that mandate some types of access but not others. The social importance of access is examined, particularly in terms of access to the information and communication technologies that are becoming so essential to everyday life. A key aspect of the discussion of information and communication technologies is the concept of accessibility, which means that technology should be designed to accommodate the needs of persons with disabilities. Part II concludes with contemporary examples of the importance of access and accessibility to persons with disabilities by investigating issues of access and accessibility related to the online environment.

Part III delves into representations of disability across media. A great deal about the social meanings of disability, the social reactions to disability, the social expectations for persons with disabilities, and the social classifications of disability can be learned from the ways in which persons with disabilities are portrayed in various media. These issues are explored in a historical sweep through disability as it has been represented in a range of media, including literature, painting, film, television, news, and advertising. The meanings of these representations, their social implications, and how they reflect social reactions to and classifications of disability are discussed. The section also reflects on the ways in which these representations have evolved and the roles persons with disabilities have played in creating these representations.

The future is the focus of part IV. Building upon the themes developed in the first three parts, this part focuses on the future of disability in society and some of the major issues that appear to be shaping the contemporary social roles of persons with disabilities. These issues include the continuing struggle for integration and inclusion, preservation and enforcement of civil rights, incorporation of issues of disability into discussions of diversity, the new medical developments that raise many concerns for persons with disabilities, and the increasing importance of access and accessibility to information and technology. Though these are not the only issues that will likely play a significant role in shaping the social future of persons with disabilities, the issues discussed in this final part are among those that seem to have the potential to have the most profound impact on the lives of persons with disabilities in the future. The text concludes with a reflection on the meaning of disability culture in a society that is not always welcoming of disability. As the movement toward rights for persons with disabilities has developed in the past several decades, so has a nascent disability culture that links persons with disabilities together. Persons with disabilities are unified not only by the social difficulties they face, but also by how they deal with these difficulties. Persons with disabilities share common experiences, some common attitudes, and even some common slang. The development of a disability culture is a hopeful sign and thus seems an appropriate way to end a book examining the social roles of disability.

Interwoven throughout all of these parts and chapters are the concepts of inclusion, access, diversity, and civil rights, which are central themes in the social lives of persons with disabilities. These concepts represent the deprivations of the past, the accomplishments and successes of the present, and the goals and needs of the future. These concepts encompass the interrelated aspects of disability in society; disability involves entwined strands of social, cultural, legal, policy, and, most important, human issues. Framing an understanding of disability are the current status of inclusion, access, diversity, and legal rights, and what must still be accomplished toward these goals. The strength of these concepts as literal and figurative frames became evident throughout the course of writing the book. Though other concepts reoccur in the text and are central to the arguments (the concept of classification is a good example), the concepts highlighted in the title fuel the progression of the text. These concepts also best reflect the positive side of the movement toward an equal place in society for persons with disabilities. In the past few decades, persons with disabilities have made a great deal of progress toward becoming included in society, gaining improved access, being accepted as part of the diverse spectrum of humankind, and establishing legal rights.

It is very important to focus on the positive aspects of the current situation of persons with disabilities in many countries. There is real reason to hope for a future where persons with disabilities are fully integrated into many, if not all, societies. Remembering the positive can be hard sometimes. There are many places on earth, perhaps still the majority, where persons with disabilities are denied the most basic of rights or considered unworthy of life. The fact that attitudes like those have changed in many societies over the past century, however, gives reason for hope. In the United States, for example, many people with disabilities born in the 1970s might have been sterilized had they been born merely a decade earlier. They likely would have also been denied any education. Had they been born in the 1920s in the United States, they might have been left to starve to death or immediately taken away from their parents and confined for life to a state institution that they would be given no option of leaving. Persons with disabilities in Europe are currently achieving integration and gaining legal rights in many areas of society. Six decades ago, many people with disabilities living in Europe were sterilized or slaughtered by the Nazis. An enormous amount of work remains before persons with disabilities have a fair and equal place in all societies, but real progress certainly has been made since the middle of the twentieth century.

The conceptual frames of this book also help to guide the reader about what the book covers. The authors' understanding of disability in society is simply one way that disability can be examined. Our perspective comes from research and teaching careers devoted to disability and lifetimes of personal experience with disability. We believe we are able to bring a broad understanding of disability to our analyses. Together and individually, we have published articles, conference papers, book chapters, and books about disability in a range of fields, including policy, education, law, information studies, literature, library studies, and disability studies. These wide-ranging research and teaching interests provide a broad lens through which to view the topic of disability in society.

In spite of the authors' scholarly and personal involvement with disability, this book is still limited. It is heavily affected by human hindrances like the inability to know and understand everything or even to be able to cover everything one knows in one text. The world is a big, complex, and usually messy place. Disability is a similarly big, complex, and usually messy topic. This concise book simply cannot touch on every corner of the globe and every possible issue related to disability. In fact, no book could. In spite of the valiant efforts of some truly dedicated historians, much of the history of persons with disabilities is permanently lost to the exclusions of the past. In many societies today, persons with disabilities are so ill regarded that their place in society does not really yet exist, making their stories lost as they occur.

Though this book focuses more on disability in more developed societies, the primary reason is that those are the societies where disability has gained the most social acceptance and persons with disabilities are able to play meaningful social roles. Disability in less developed societies is certainly not bypassed in this text, however. The issues related to disability in technologically advanced societies also point more toward the future issues of disability in society. The rise of the age of information and the accompanying omnipresence of information and communication technologies like computers and the Internet creates many new and often unforeseen issues for people with disabilities. A fairly insignificant, yet not atypical, example of how new technologies almost always create new problems for people with disabilities are the increasingly common boxes at checkout lanes for credit and debit card purchases. The customer puts the card in the little machine, enters some information pressing buttons on the screen, signs the screen, and the transaction is completed. These devices are a great convenience for most customers. For persons with visual impairments, these devices are basically not usable. The screens are not large, there is little contrast between the text and the background on the screen, and they lack voice capacity. For people who cannot use the devices because they cannot read them, there is no convenience factor. Instead, they create problems and obstacles, as the needs of customers with visual impairments were apparently never considered in the design of these devices. A small bit of trouble in the grand scheme of things, but multiply such troubles by all of the new information and communication technologies that are becoming a part of virtually every aspect of daily life.

This book presents an exploration of disability in society and social roles of persons with disabilities. It is based on many years of research and two lifetimes of personal experience. Discussions and dialogues with many students, colleagues, and friends with disabilities inform the book. It approaches disability comprehensively by drawing from and linking together thinking about disability from a diverse range of areas of scholarship that are usually not bridged. The book examines disability as human, social, cultural, legal, and policy issues that encompass concepts like inclusion, access, diversity, and legal rights. Ultimately, this book offers a framework for understanding disability in society—where we are, how we got here, where we are headed, and the issues that must be addressed as we go forward in the age of information.

I

The Social Lives of Disability

1

The Roles of Disability in Society

The first part of this book explores the evolution of the social roles of disability, tracing their history from ancient times into the present information age. This part will, hopefully, provide a range of insights into the social meanings of disability and the importance of understanding these social issues in any aggregation of interdependent individuals who coexist in an organized community. Across societies throughout most of human history, having a disability meant being a social outcast or much worse, though the situation has finally begun to change. In the past few decades, persons with disabilities in the United States and in many other nations have experienced considerable changes in the extent to which they are included in society. In the United States, for example, antidiscrimination laws have opened up education, employment, the political system, the judicial system, and many other major parts of society to individuals with disabilities. Many individuals with disabilities have witnessed and experienced significant changes to cultural attitudes about disability in their lifetimes. In the past three decades, as a result of changes in the law, in the attitudes of people with disabilities, and in society, individuals with disabilities have experienced a change in the way they are treated and the ways in which they are able to participate in society. Though persons with disabilities still face enormous problems of misunderstanding and discrimination, real progress has been made and continues to occur.

When I received my PhD, I went to visit my grandparents in their retirement home in central Florida to share the excitement of completing a terminal degree and securing a wonderful university teaching position. They were extremely proud of my accomplishments and giggled like silly teenagers as they used the title "Dr." before my name. Still, when a neighbor came over to visit with my grandparents, my grandfather introduced me by saying, "Phil, I'd like you to meet my crippled granddaughter."

Changes in societal attitudes are reflected by the accepted terms used to describe people with disabilities. The change has been away from equating the person with his or her impairment to describing the person as having an impairment. Until recently, it was socially acceptable to refer to a person with a disability as lame, crippled, retarded, handicapped (derived from "cap in hand," an old English term for begging), or even defective. The importance of language may be best understood by comparing the implications of using the term "disabled person" as opposed to "person with a disability." The first term places the emphasis on the disability, whereas the second term places the emphasis on the person, which is frequently described as "person-first" terminology. The use of person-first terminology linguistically reinforces that the person is more than, and more important than, the disability. The general shift toward using more humane terms to describe the condition of having a disability has been fueled by members of the disability community asserting their right to be treated as human beings.

The terminology related to particular disabilities has also changed mightily, further reflecting an emphasis on the person rather than the impairment. Persons who use wheelchairs used to be commonly referred to as "wheelchair bound," while persons with hearing impairments were commonly referred to as "deaf and dumb." This latter term was both offensive and inaccurate, as persons with hearing impairments were often incorrectly assumed to be unable to speak. Both of these terms highlight an inability and make the individual sound close to helpless by using limiting terms like "bound" and "dumb." The terms that are now commonly used for the same conditions, "wheelchair user" and "hearing impaired," acknowledge the disability without implying that the individual is rendered helpless by it. A person may use a wheelchair, but that person can do most anything he or she wants. A person may have a hearing impairment, but he or she can communicate ideas and express feelings as well as any other person.

Changes in commonly used terms may not seem revolutionary, but they reflect and reinforce slowly evolving social attitudes toward persons with disabilities. The changes have been furthered by the writing of scholarly and popular personal narratives by people with disabilities, as well as by the appearance of magazines, Web sites, and other publications devoted to issues of disability (Rapp & Ginsburg, 2001). These publications have helped to increase awareness of issues of disability, to personalize disability for people who had not previously put a human face on it, and to increase public support for disability rights (Rapp & Ginsburg, 2001). There is power in an individual's personal story, and personal stories can have great ability to affect social change (Stewart, 2000).

> A graduate student asked if she could miss class one evening. When I asked why, she told me that she and her husband recently became parents and their new son was diagnosed with Down syndrome. They had not been prepared for any medical problems and she wanted to attend a support group for parents of Down syndrome children. I told her to definitely go and asked her if she would then share what she had learned. When she came into class the following week, she looked radiant and more carefree. Before I even asked, she told the entire class about the people she met and shared several personal stories about her son. The stories she had heard put all the medical information she had been given into a human, a real, perspective. Her son did not have to be a case number for the occupational therapist or a statistic for the pediatrician. She heard hopeful—and hurtful—stories that gave her understanding and strength.

Disability is part of the "natural physical, social, and cultural variability of the human species" (Scotch & Schriner, 1997, p. 154). Disability is a cross-cultural phenomenon, having been present in every human culture (Scheer & Groce, 1988). The variations in types of disabilities reflect other types of variations in people (Higgins, 1992; Sheer & Groce, 1988; Zola, 1993). People with disabilities, however, still face considerable prejudice in many facets of daily life, as evidenced by many different commonplace experiences. Prejudice drives the still considerable sources of exclusion and helps determine the levels of access that a society allows individuals with disabilities. Prejudice plays a sizeable role in how people with disabilities are classified by society and in how persons with disabilities are represented in media. Prejudice also fuels the ways in which many members of society react to individuals with disabilities. Many people still regard persons with disabilities in terms of a range of stereotyping and oppressive perceptions, particularly feigned concern, sentimentality, in-difference, or outright hostility (Thomas, 1982). The move toward social integration must be considered in light of the fact that integration for persons with disabilities still does not mean being considered an integral aspect of a society (Stiker, 1999). Subsequent chapters in this part discuss the roles of disability through time and examine the historical impacts of social classifi-cation, access, civil rights, and social reactions in shaping the evolving social roles of individuals with disabilities.

Prior to delving further into these specific issues, it is important to consider the meaning of the word "disability" in society. In a very real way, this entire book is an exploration of the social meaning of the term "disability." However, it is important to begin examining disability by thinking about what it means to be considered a person with a disability. Suggested definitions of disability vary widely and can be rooted in medical, social, or economic factors. Many defi-nitions link disability directly to an identifiable medical impairment or condition that impacts that daily life. Other approaches include conceiving of disability as a process (Baldwin, 1997) or an interaction (Brandt & Pope, 1997). Disability can be thought of as a "yes-no proposition" or as a continuum of differing abilities (Cunningham & Coombs, 1997, p. 145). The simple fact is that defining disability is a complex process.

Disability, unlike most other characteristics, is not a static, unchanging, or immutable condition. Most people who have a disability were not born with it, making it very different from characteristics like gender. Disability can manifest as a physical or cognitive issue, coming from a range of factors—genetics, accident, external circumstances, or advancing age. People with disabilities are not unified by national origin, skin color, or language. In some cases, medical or technological advances can even eliminate a disability. Some people who have disabilities argue that they do not have one. The ways in which a disability will affect a particular individual are related to numerous variables, such as time of onset of disability, type of onset, what bodily functions are involved, severity, visibility, stability, and the amount of accompanying pain (Vash & Crewe, 2004). In short, it can be very difficult to establish a comprehensive definition of disability that accounts for the full range of conditions and impacts.

In a previous work, we posited that persons with disabilities could be identified by the presence of two unifying and interrelated factors: (1) having an ongoing physical or mental condition that society deems unusual, and (2) facing discrimination and exclusion as a result of having a condition that society deems unusual (Jaeger & Bowman, 2002, pp. 17–25). This definition, though far from perfect, seems reasonable enough as a starting point for this book. This definition places much of the nexus on the social attitudes toward persons with disabilities. Such emphasis is key for thinking about disability in terms of society, since disabilities are labeled as such by other members of a society. Disability exists in society because certain conditions are thought by the majority of members of the society to be far enough from the norm that they significantly affect daily activities in some way.

For example, imagine a society that inverts the social positions of people who use wheelchairs and those who do not. In a society where the majority of people were wheelchair users and everything was designed to meet their needs, the people who would be "disabled" would be those who did not use wheelchairs. A person not in a wheelchair would find buildings hard to get into, doorways too short, things placed at an inconveniently low height, and many other problems that someone in a wheelchair would not likely think about. Stairs and chairs would be considered accommodations. The types of conditions that are deemed disabilities say as much about the values of the society as about the medical conditions of the individuals.

After completing college, Miguel was surprised by some of the experiences he had trying to find his first job. Though his visual impairment had prevented him from doing many things throughout his life, he had never had problems accomplishing his work in school or in part-time jobs he had held. In one particularly odd interview, Miguel was abruptly told that he could not fill the requirements of the job almost as soon as he sat down. Miguel noted that he actually did have every qualification the ad listed. He was told that they could never hire someone with vision problems because the company thought it was important for all employees to be able to take clients golfing.

The way in which a society defines disability is reflected in social attitudes and, more recently, in legal definitions of disability. As the next three chapters explore, disability is very much a social issue. The ways in which members of a society classify and react to disability have a profound impact on the lives of persons with disabilities. The ways in which a society chooses to legally define disability have a tremendous impact on the social standing and civil rights of persons with disabilities. These social classifications, social reactions, and legal classifications are interrelated and serve to reinforce the definitions for and social roles of disability.

2

Social Classifications of and Reactions to Disability

Historian Daniel J. Boorstin has described areas of history that do not receive considerable discussion or study as "hidden history," the parts of human experience that are forgotten or relegated to peripheral status (Boorstin, 1989, p. xi). Much of the history of individuals with disabilities, their roles in society, and their own cultural attributes undoubtedly could be considered hidden history. Disability is "conspicuously absent in the histories we write. When historians do take note of disability, they usually treat it merely as personal tragedy or as an insult to be deplored and a label to be denied, rather than as a cultural construct to be questioned and explored" (Baynton, 2001, p. 52). Sadly, many discussions of history and society that do include issues of disability actually demonstrate a bias against disability by the author (Edwards, 1997).

Whether this peripheral status results from discomfort, ignorance, or prejudice, individuals with disabilities have been rarely studied or noted over time. In spite of the fact that disability has been present throughout history, historians rarely study disability beyond medical case histories (Longmore & Umansky, 2001). As history has been written primarily by those who do not have disabilities, social concepts about disability have been greatly shaped by people who have no experience with disability (Morris, 1991). Such lack of understanding of disability is evident throughout society. A tangible example is the preeminence of stairs, revealing social discounting of those who cannot walk and the fact that most architects do not think seriously about access for persons with disabilities (Gleeson, 1999; Siebers, 2001).

The lack of understanding of disability has also extended through research about disability in the sciences, social sciences, and humanities (Longmore, 2003). Only with the rise of the disability rights movement in the late twentieth century have individuals with disabilities become a more mainstream presence in society and in scholarship. This increase in social presence has been directly linked to the painfully slow march toward legal rights for individuals with disabilities. Despite gaining a greater role in society and rights under the law, persons with disabilities are still separated in many ways not only from mainstream society but from other minority groups. "Concepts of citizenship, the economy, and the body are embedded in understandings of what constitutes well-being, understandings that generally exclude or marginalize the forms or realities of disability" (Breckenridge & Vogler, 2001, p. 351). The seemingly permanent outsider status of individuals with disabilities, from the remotest points in the past to the present day, raises one very obvious question. Specifically, what is the reason for this consistent exclusion? A large part of the answer is tied to how a society classifies persons with disabilities.

SOCIAL CLASSIFICATIONS OF DISABILITY

Classifications are used by a society "to raise explanation to the level of generalization" about a group (Bates & Peacock, 1989, p. 572). Social classifications encompass the beliefs, assumptions, and stereotypes by members of a society that create a generally accepted set of social perceptions about a particular group of people within the society. Classifications are necessarily broad mental boxes into which items are categorized and separated. "Our lives are henged round with systems of classifications" (Bowker & Star, 1999, p. 1). Classifications are a natural human function that can be very helpful. Classifications allow us to make useful distinctions, like the difference between a fluffy bunny and an irate hippopotamus or the difference between a toaster and a washcloth. In many ways, classifications facilitate most life activities. Without classifications, all the papers on our desks or in our filing cabinets would be in random order and very hard to use. Classifications help set social roles and accompanying actions when dealing with types of individuals with established social functions. These classifications, for example, help us avoid confusing the social function of a police officer with that of a chef.

People also use classifications to establish perceived social roles for groups of people with some type of similarity. When many people in a society share similar social classifications of a particular group of people, that society develops specific ways of treating that group. An unfortunate example of such classifications is socially specified roles for people with different skin colors (Bowker & Star, 1999). Ultimately, classifications in the real world "intimately interpenetrate" the lives of the people they classify (Bowker & Star, 1999, p. 163).

Across cultures, social classifications of disability have driven the marginalization, disempowerment, and exclusion of persons with disabilities. Bowker and Star (1999) describe the classification of disabling conditions, using tuberculosis as an example, as "the interweaving of myth, biography, science, medicine, and bureaucracy" (p. 165). The classification of disability is very complex due to the differences in the manifestations of the disability, the course it takes, the patient's personal experience with the disability, the reactions of others, the way the disability has been studied by doctors, and many other factors. A person with a disability may also differ with the medical profession or others about how his or her disability is classified. The classification of one disability "does not stand alone," as it is also inscribed into the greater discourse of the classification of all disabilities (Bowker & Star, 1999, p. 173). Disabilities ultimately create many commonalities both in the experiences of the individuals with the conditions and in how they are treated and classified by others (Ziporyn, 1992).

Although individuals develop personalized constructions of reality, their perceptions are heavily influenced by historical and cultural factors (Ferrante, 1988). The social construction of a group, particularly a marginalized group, will shape the way members of that group are viewed and treated by others (Huber & Gillaspy, 1998). For persons with disabilities, these social constructions have greatly influenced the social and legal classifications of disability throughout history. These classifications have led to the present situation in the United States, where disability has several formal legal classifications and many informal social classifications. Social classifications are filtered through personal perceptions, since people think about disability in different ways based on individual background and personal understanding of the meaning of disability (Turnbull & Stowe, 2001).

> For one semester I was coteaching a fifth grade class every Thursday. The 23 11-year-olds were a delight to interact with and every week brought new discussions, readings, projects, and activities. It was apparent that the students looked forward to my arrival, as there was always a welcoming committee on the school steps. One afternoon a mother came to pick her child up for a dental appointment. As I extended my hand in greeting, she said, "My son talks about you constantly. We always hear what books you have brought to class and what you tell the students. I hope this doesn't offend you, but none of the students ever mentioned your disability."

"To a large extent, disability is a social construct" (Schmetzke, 2002, p. 135), and this social construct can have a profound impact on individuals with disabilities. The "intimate classifications" of people with disabilities can have tremendous impacts on those individuals, infiltrating and influencing many aspects of their lives (Bowker & Star, 1999, p. 163). In general, individuals with disabilities have been socially classified as outsiders throughout history, with differing cultures constructing radically different classifications of disability as outsider. A common factor to almost all social classifications of disability is the presence of discriminatory attitudes. These classifications reveal ongoing attitudes toward persons with disabilities and assumptions that are considered to be social norms.

As long as disability has been present in a society, members of that society have made judgments about its meaning (Albrecht, 1992). Over time, the social classifications have included viewing individuals with disabilities as evidence of the wrath of a supernatural power, as a prophetic sign of negative future events, as useless objects, as amusement, as fodder for public sport, and as suffers of demonic possession (Bragg, 1997; French, 1932; Hibbert, 1975; Rosen, 1968; Stone, 1999; Warkany, 1959). In colonial times in the United States, individuals with disabilities were often classified in terms of the people who were socially expected to support them (Bryan, 1996). As Western societies began to articulate cultural standards for normalcy, these definitions usually juxtaposed normalcy with disability (Davis, 1997, 2000). More than anything else, individuals with disabilities have been consistently classified as having little social value or as not part of society at all (Baynton, 2001; Bessis, 1995; Braddock & Parish, 2001). Overall, the history of disability has predominantly been one of social exclusion, and the classifications of disability have reinforced this exclusion.

Regardless of the time period or the society, disability has tended to function as a "master status," a classification that has more social import than anything else in defining an individual (Albrecht & Verbugge, 2000, p. 301). The classification of disability "floods all statuses and identities" of a person, so that "a woman who uses a wheelchair because of multiple sclerosis becomes a disabled mother, handicapped driver, disabled worker, and wheelchair dancer" (Charmaz, 2000, p. 284). The fact that disability is a master status offers some explanation as to why persons with disabilities remain outsiders to other social minority groups. A woman with a disability is mainly perceived by others in terms of her disability, not her gender. Similarly, others usually perceive a male Latino business executive with a disability as being disabled first, and everything else is secondary.

The master status role of disability also creates resistance to any facets of a person's life that confound the classification of "disabled." For many people who do not have a disability, the social classification of disability is so powerful that a person with a disability is not expected to engage in any activities that evidence personal empowerment or self-sufficiency. Although many people who use wheelchairs do not use them all the time, there is a social expectation that a person in a wheelchair is always in a wheelchair. The person has been socially classified as having a disability, and anything that interrupts that classification, such as the person using crutches, disturbs others' classifications of the person as being just a person with a disability. A social classification of disability is truly a classification of disempowerment.

The classifications of disability can have far-reaching impacts on an individual's life. People with disabilities have "far lower incomes than other citizens"

(National Council on Disability, 2001, p. 103). In the United States, in spite of the passage of laws to protect the rights of persons with disabilities, approximately one quarter of people with disabilities are employed, and 75 percent of those who are not employed "would like to work but cannot find employment" (Dispenza, 2002, p. 160). The average rate of unemployment for adults with disabilities tends to be around 70 percent, while the unemployment rate for other adults tends to be around 5 percent (Rich, Erb, & Rich, 2002). Since 1990, the employment rates for persons with disabilities have fallen, as general employment rates have held steady or increased (Bound & Waidmann, 2002). The unemployment of persons with disabilities under age sixty-five tends to be higher than the total unemployment rate of any other nation (Charlton, 1998). Overall, people with disabilities are much more likely to live in poverty and are less likely to have adequate access to education, health care, and housing than other members of society (Rich et al., 2002).

Sally has an MBA. She graduated near the top of her class and has sterling recommendations from her professors. While in business school, her knowledge and creativity were the envy of her classmates. She has been unable to find work using her degree in the two years since she graduated from business school. Whenever she goes to an interview, Sally finds that she is not what the employer expected from her resume. Though she has a hearing impairment, it does not affect her ability to work. Unfortunately, potential employers do not seem to be able to look beyond the hearing aids and the fact that her speech sounds a little different. Though the interviewers never say that she will not be hired due to her disability, she is always informed before she leaves that she does not fit the needs of the company.

The social classifications of individuals with disabilities that have the most profound impact on the present may be those that arose from the eugenics movement. The movement known as eugenics, which was based on the principle that people with disabilities should not be allowed to reproduce, became popular in the late nineteenth century and early twentieth century in the United States and many other nations. Most states had laws mandating the institutionalization or sterilization of individuals with various disabilities. Along with the United States, other nations that passed eugenics laws included the United Kingdom, Australia, and many nations of continental Europe (Baker, 2002). The Supreme Court of the United States upheld the legality of such laws so that the United States would not be "swamped with incompetence" and to "prevent those who are manifestly unfit from continuing their kind" (*Buck v. Bell*, 1927, p. 207).

The sterilization laws of California actually became the model for the laws passed in Nazi Germany that led to the sterilization of as many as 400,000 people and the subsequent murder of at least 200,000 individuals with disabilities in the 1930s and 1940s in Europe (Reilly, 1991). Britain also passed laws similar to those of California (MacKenzie, 1981), and the prestigious scientific journal *Science* ran an editorial in 1933 lauding these efforts, advocating the sterilization of those with mental impairments, many emotional illnesses, visual impairments, auditory impairments, and various bodily malformations (Davis, 1997). The legacy of these laws can still be felt in the social and legal classifications of individuals with disabilities in many nations around the world (Garton, 2000; Lowe, 2000).

THEORETICAL PERSPECTIVES ON DISABILITY

Disabilities, and the knowledge related to disabilities, "co-exist within a social reality" (Huber & Gillaspy, 1998, p. 190). Many academic fields have relied very heavily on the equation of the disability with the person, making the individual with the disability seem to be either a problem or of negligible value. Sociologists, for example, typically ignore disability or only study it as something exotic (Barton, 1996). When disability is studied and discussed theoretically, it is often in offensive ways (Hahn, 1997), as many researchers view disability only in terms of a biological condition that leaves the person in need of assistance (Fine & Asch, 1988). Many individuals with disabilities view much of the research on disability as reflecting and perpetuating negative social myths and stereotypes (Kitchin, 2000; Stone & Priestly, 1996). Given that disability can be studied from many different perspectives, such as human development, public policy, law, culture, society, ethics, philosophy, and technology (Turnbull & Stowe, 2001), the failure to better account for disability is all the more problematic.

Research about disability has produced a number of theoretical perspectives to try to explain disability in society. Though these perspectives do not directly address issues of classification, they certainly can be very helpful when thinking about classification of disability. The different approaches to identifying the roots and causes of disability offer a menu of options for considering the origins of social classifications of disability. These perspectives approach disability as a medical issue, a social issue, an economic issue, and a postmodern issue.

In society and in research, the individual with a disability is often viewed in terms of the disability, and the disability is often seen as a purely medical issue that can and should be treated. The *medical perspective* emphasizes that the disability is a biological or physiological function within the person (Silvers, 1998). The medical perspective classifies disability entirely within the person with a disability, removed from any external factors. Under this socially conservative perspective, problems due to disability are considered to reside in the individual independently of social context, identifying the individual with the disability as a biological problem. The goal for disability, then, is to find medical cures to eliminate disability. Simultaneously, this perspective focuses on disability as a problem that, through medical and technological advances, can be eradicated (Switzer, 2003). The eugenics movement is the quintessential medical approach to disability.

This medical emphasis has had a great impact on the way disability is classified and described by society at large. Such research focuses on how "to define and describe the malady, classify the pathological, and provide discourse regarding affected individuals" (Huber & Gillaspy, 1998, p. 201). The medical perspective has shaped many classifications of disability in the medical community and in the general public through approach and through terminology, fostering negative perceptions of persons with disabilities. The "medical language of disability soon became the social language of insult and disparagement.... [These terms] have lost their original medical connotations and become cultural tools to devalue and marginalize specific groups of people" (Christensen, 1996, p. 64).

These embedded cultural notions of the medical perspective also extend to social institutions. Written policies on disability from social institutions "tend to offer justification of the status quo" (Riddell, 1996, p. 83). In an attempt to directly address these problems created by the medical perspective, scholars who study disability issues have created a number of other perspectives to try to better understand disability in society. These perspectives have arisen in reaction to failure of the scholarly mainstream to adequately study and discuss disability in society (Bowman & Jaeger, 2003).

The *social perspective* of disability asserts that "disability is the outcome of social arrangements which work to restrict the activities of people with impairments by placing social barriers in their way" (Thomas, 1999, p. 14). A disability, according to the social perspective, is the result of how a physical or mental characteristic affects functioning in an environment and the expectations for functioning (Silvers, 1998, 2000). In sharp contrast to the medical perspective, the social perspective views disability more as a result of external factors imposed upon a person than the biological functions of a person. The social perspective "makes it possible to see disability as the effect of an environment hostile to some bodies and not others, requiring advances in social justice rather than in medicine" (Siebers, 2001, p. 738). Beliefs and functions that marginalize and disempower persons with disabilities can then be seen as impediments to living to the fullest of their abilities. The social perspective focuses on "citizenship rights and the way in which social organizations oppress disabled people" (Marks, 1999, p. 77). This perspective works to make clear social prejudices in order to promote acceptance of the range of disabilities to create a more inclusive view of humankind.

Under the social perspective, discrimination against individuals with disabilities, which is sometimes identified as disablism, is viewed as similar to sexism, racism, homophobia, and ageism as oppressions of particular groups based on social, political, and economic forces (Abberly, 1987). The social perspective holds that the goal should be to reduce the disadvantages created by an impairment in order to ensure equality for all persons (Silvers, 1998). Although possible deficiencies in the social perspective of disability have been noted (Corker & French, 1999; Thomas, 1999), it seems to remain the most prominent, or at least most commonly discussed, perspective on the social classification of disability among persons with disabilities.

Some scholars have focused on specific issues within the social perspective as extremely important. One approach emphasizes the role of labels in the social construction of disability, seeing disability as a "negative social label that is applied by some people to others with the effect of enforcing social marginalisation" (Riddell, 1996, p. 86). This perspective views disability as a direct creation of the social exclusion through the external imposition of labels through means of laws, policies, and social standards. Other scholars have asserted the importance of social functions in the social construction of disability. This view maintains that disability results from classifications specifically of social organizations and state agencies (Albrecht, 1992; Stone, 1984). From this approach, disability is not a product of medical, social, or political classifications, but is a result of the ways in which individuals with disabilities are treated by the institutions of that society.

Rather than viewing disability as a medical or social issue, some scholars conceive of disability as an economic issue. The *materialist perspective* asserts that the oppression of people with disabilities is rooted in economic terms, neither within the individual nor within the attitudes of others (Barnes, 1990; Finkelstein, 1980; Oliver, 1990). According to the materialist perspective, impairments are not social constructs but instead have tangible economic causes, such as professional vested interests, technological change, and economic priorities. In this view, a person with a disability is less valued as a worker by employers, is viewed as a constraint by other workers, and is perceived as having greater difficulty dealing with new technology. All of these factors contribute to attitudes that serve to marginalize persons with disabilities for economic reasons. This perspective views the main problem as being the perception of individuals with disabilities as having lower economic worth than other members of society.

Taking a different track than all other perspectives on disability, the *postmodernist perspectives* question the value of trying to create a theory of disability since human experience is too varied and complex to be accommodated by theory (Shakespeare, 1994). Since there are so many individual experiences and personal accounts due to factors like gender, race, and type of disability, it may be impossible to theoretically classify the parameters of the experiences faced by individuals with disabilities. Disability has also been studied specifically in terms of postmodernist viewpoints from feminist perspectives (Lonsdale, 1990; Thomas, 1999), racial perspectives (McDonald, 1991; Stuart, 1992), and queer theory perspectives (McRuer, 2003; Samuels, 2003), among others. Each of these approaches attempts to create an understanding of disability in terms of a portion of the population of persons with disabilities, such as persons with disabilities who are also African American.

These multiple and divergent views all contribute to trying to better understand the social classification of disability. When examining social classifications that are discussed throughout this book, it is important to reflect upon the causes of those classifications, which may be rooted in medical, social, economic, or very idiosyncratic reasons. Sometimes the relationship is clear; the people who believed in eugenics clearly thought of disability as a purely medical problem that had to be eliminated. In many other cases, however, several or all of these perspectives on disability will feed into a classification.

Consider, for example, the decision by an employer not to hire someone who is fully qualified for a job simply because the job applicant is a wheelchair user. The employer may fear unforeseen medical problems that the applicant's condition may cause. The employer may fear the economic costs of making modifications and accommodations that will allow the applicant to do the job. The employer may have bias against persons with disabilities as a result of common social attitudes. In many cases, the employer will actually have all of these opinions, blurring the distinctions between the medical, social, and economic perspectives. The end result is that the employer is classifying the applicant as incapable as an employee, regardless of talent or qualification, for the single fact that the applicant uses a wheelchair. As such, though these perspectives help to better understand how the disability is socially classified, these perspectives alone will not lead to an understanding of the complex position of persons with disabilities in society or how to facilitate greater inclusion of individuals with disabilities into society.

As the example above indicates, the marginalization and exclusion of individuals with disabilities are inextricably linked to classifications of disability, regardless of whether those classifications are rooted in medical, social, or economic perspectives. The ways in which disability is classified by a society also lead to the social reactions that many people who do not have disabilities display around the people who do. Social reactions to disability result from the social classifications of disability, as the classifications create certain expectations and accepted ways to treat persons with disabilities within a society. People who do not have disabilities often rely on these established classifications as their frame of acceptable behavior when interacting with a person with a disability.

SOCIAL REACTIONS TO DISABILITY

Even when a society is not intentionally discriminating against individuals with disabilities, the members of that society may be marginalizing people with disabilities through their social reactions to disability that are built upon the social classifications of disability. These social reactions include ignoring, stereotyping, misidentification, and discomfort. One writer noted, "the problem of disability lies not only in the impairment of function and its effects on us individually, but also, more importantly, in the area of our relationship with 'normal' people" (Hunt, 1966, p. 146). Another individual encapsulated the importance of social reactions by noting, "My disability is how people respond to my disability" (Frank, 1988, p. 111). Each of the social reactions to disability is evidenced in a different way, but all reveal an intent, conscious or not, to marginalize and disempower individuals with disabilities. Persons with disabilities can truly be regarded as "twice marginalized" in society—by anxiety and discomfort felt by others and by the tendency to dismiss disability as anything more than a medical issue (Breckenridge & Vogler, 2001, p. 349). Many people with disabilities genuinely believe having a disability is made most difficult by "society's myths, fears, and stereotypes" (Shapiro, 1993, p. 5).

The central problem is that it can be very hard to understand disability if one has neither experienced a disability nor been close to someone else who has a disability. People unfamiliar with disability often simply have never thought about or made the effort to try to learn about life with a disability. Astoundingly, many people in the United States form their attitudes about disability based on the portrayals of persons with disabilities in telethons and other charitable functions (Charlton, 1998). As a result, people who do not have disabilities often have only the socially accepted classifications of persons with disabilities to draw upon when interacting with them. Most people who lack experience with disability have no idea that people with disabilities can face daily discriminations and indignities like being asked to leave places because they appear offensive, having to use separate entrances and facilities, or being treated as if they cannot speak for themselves. Persons with disabilities also face the strange problem of being called names that have become commonplace and reflexive social metaphors for anything negative, like "lame," "blind," and "retarded" (Lacheen, 2000, p. 243). Though every person has individual experiences with disability and each disability comes with its own set of struggles, persons with disabilities are united by how they are classified by society and by the ways in which they are treated in society.

> My best friend in college married a man from her hometown, a man I had never met. Even though I was a bridesmaid in her wedding, even though I had known her family for years, her husband would never join us in social activities. When I asked her why, she replied honestly that he was uncomfortable with me—he pitied me—and it made him uncomfortable to be around me.

The most basic social reaction to disability may be to pretend that it is not there. Of course, pretending disability does not exist also means pretending that people with disabilities do not exist. Ignoring disability occurs in all aspects of society, from daily interactions to history texts. In fact, history texts provide innumerable examples of disability being ignored to the extent that, if you did not know otherwise, you would never assume that individuals with disabilities ever existed. Even many texts that claim to represent a "people's history" or a history of previously underrepresented voices make no mention of persons with disabilities; apparently, they are the history of all peoples except individuals with disabilities. The failure to acknowledge disability by many writers of history reflects the social attitude that allows the ignoring of people with disabilities.

It is in everyday occurrences that individuals with disabilities most frequently experience being ignored. The experiences can entail trying to talk to someone who will only converse with a person you are with, or simply not being acknowledged at all by a clerk in a store. The ignoring can occur when a parent tells a child not to look at you when you go by or when someone refers to you only in terms of your disability. The conscious desire to be distanced from persons with disabilities is particularly curious when compared to social reactions to other minority groups. Many people who will never directly benefit from racial equality (i.e., whites), gender equity (i.e., men), or gay rights (i.e., heterosexuals) still openly and actively support these causes. However, very few people who do not have a disability actively support causes of disability rights, even though many people who do not now have a disability will have one in the future (Berube, 1997).

The act of distancing from individuals with disabilities as a social phenomenon has been studied for nearly half a century. Early studies (Goffman, 1963; Kleck, Ono, & Hastorf, 1966; Richardson, 1963) found, not surprisingly, that people who do not have disabilities generally tend to be uncomfortable around persons with disabilities. Later studies began to discover that people tend to react with different levels of discomfort around people with different types of disabilities, and that the reactions to a particular disability tended to be very similar across a wide range of people (Horne & Ricciardo, 1988; Jones, 1974; Tringo, 1970). Studies also found that teachers and other students generally held similar negative attitudes toward students with disabilities (Horne, 1985). People tend to show a hierarchy of reactions to disability, with certain types of disabilities being seen as more acceptable, or less distressing, than others (Grand, Bernier, & Strohmer, 1982; Harasymiw, Horne, & Lewis, 1976; Schneider & Anderson, 1980; Westbrook, Legge, & Pennay, 1993). The disabilities that people were less likely to distance themselves from were those perceived to still allow the person with the disability to be socially and economically productive or were more common conditions, and therefore respondents were likely to know someone with that condition, such as heart disease or cancer (Horne & Ricciardo, 1988; Tringo, 1970).

Anna is an elementary school student who has juvenile rheumatoid arthritis. The way her condition makes her feel varies from day to day. On good days, she can walk short distances; on bad days, she needs to use a wheelchair. The teachers at Anna's school are having a hard time understanding how some days she can walk and other days she cannot do. In fact, many of the teachers at the school have openly said that they think Anna is pretending to be unable to walk. As a result, her teachers often try to make Anna do things she physically cannot. Anna's parents have protested this treatment, but the principal of the school has sided with the teachers, saying that if she can walk one day, she can walk every day.

The social distancing of persons with disabilities often leads to completely ignoring them. Ignoring people with disabilities can even occur when no one with a disability is present. For example, not too many years ago, a large political demonstration to support affirmative action was occurring on a major university campus. One of the organizers of the event parked a car in a space reserved for individuals with disabilities. This organizer had no disability and, as a result, had no right to park in the space. So the organizer of the rally to protect the rights of one socially disadvantaged group acted to ignore the existence of another disadvantaged group, people with disabilities. In fact, parking spaces for individuals with disabilities can be seen as an encapsulation of ignoring the needs of persons with disabilities even when making an attempt to create accommodations, as these parking spaces are often put in hard-to-reach places or are far from doors (Siebers, 2003). Parallel problems often occur in public schools, as students with disabilities are integrated into general education classrooms but still treated as outsiders to the rest of the class and removed from many of the activities of the classroom (Ware, 2002).

As a social reaction, stereotyping happens to people in many diverse social groups. People with disabilities, however, face extremely significant problems with stereotyping, particularly from people who lack firsthand experience interacting with persons with disabilities. Though stereotypes rarely have any direct relation to the way a particular individual really is, stereotypes can radically alter interpersonal interactions, as the person believing the stereotype may be unable to view the person as anything but the stereotype. This dynamic makes the stereotype a self-fulfilling prophecy whereby persons with disabilities cannot be viewed beyond the stereotype. The stereotyping of disability, for both persons with disabilities and those without, is shaped in the earliest educational experiences when students with disabilities take certain different classes or attend different schools (Linton, 1998a).

The presence of a disability "frequently short circuits the normal exchange of information and impressions about another person" (Colker & Tucker, 1998, p. 5). Individuals with disabilities are often stereotyped as socially stigmatized, as objects of pity, as something less than human, as eternal innocents, or as sources of inspiration, both in society and in representations of society, such as literature and art (Black, 2004; Bowman & Jaeger, 2003, 2004). In the local laws of many cities in the nineteenth and early twentieth centuries, these stigmas were institutionalized in municipal codes known as "ugly laws" (Burgdorf & Burgdorf, 1976). Many American cities had such laws, and they mandated that persons who were maimed or disfigured or otherwise physically different were not allowed to be in public view in community areas and public spaces like sidewalks, parks, and public buildings (Burgdorf & Burgdorf, 1976; Siebers, 2003).

Another problematic social reaction to disability is misidentification, an odd by-product of the increase in legal rights of people with disabilities. Some people see having a disability as a means of personal gain, whether for advantage, for convenience, or to gain sympathy. Anyone with an obvious disability has had the strange experience of being told by a perfectly healthy individual that he or she also has a disability, such as having to wear contacts, being prone to getting rashes, having trouble remembering birthdays, being lactose intolerant, having allergies to cats, sneezing when they smell lilacs, or innumerable other idiotic complaints that people inexplicably misidentify as disabilities. Why people do so may derive from the attention that can be garnered by sounding full of woe and self-pity. Saying you deserve pity is a much less difficult way to gain attention than having an appealing personality or being a decent person. Though misidentifying an insignificant problem as a disability may get attention from some people, it has negative social consequences beyond insulting people who actually have disabilities. The ultimate result is confusion in society as to what a disability really is.

Discomfort is another very common social reaction to disability. People who do not have disabilities often feel uncertain how to act when encountering someone with a disability, though spending time around persons with disabilities can reduce these feelings of uncertainty (Albrecht, Walker, & Levy, 1982; Zahn, 1973). The inexperience of many people in interacting with persons with disabilities often leads to discomfort and awkwardness in interactions. Every person with a disability has had countless conversations that were stilted or ineffective because the other person felt uncomfortable because of the disability. The person was focusing exclusively on the presence of a disability rather than the presence of someone with a disability.

Social discomfort around persons with disabilities can also result from what has been described as aesthetic anxiety arising from another's physical appearance and existential anxiety arising from the fear of loss triggered by encountering someone who experiences some sort of loss (Hahn, 1983, 1988; Livneh, 1982). Existential anxiety stems from the fear of having a disability one day and the fear that a disability would interfere with the current quality of life (Hahn, 1988). This sort of anxiety can also lead people to be so uncomfortable that they assume persons with disabilities are somehow at fault for having a disability (Vash & Crewe, 2004). Aesthetic anxiety is tied to devaluation of those who do not conform to standard body images in society and to the social tendency to subordinate those who are different (Hahn, 1988), including differences in appearance, movement, function, and communication (Olkin & Howson, 1994). Some people are so uncomfortable that they become paralyzed with fear around anyone with a disability. A large number of these reactions involve an inability to see past the disability, but they also have much to do with a lack of time spent around people with disabilities.

Social discomfort around persons with disabilities is not a one-way street, however, as persons with disabilities are sometimes uncomfortable around people who do not have disabilities (Richardson, 1963). Persons with disabilities may at times not know whether to acknowledge their own disabilities in the presence of people who do not have disabilities (Levitin, 1975; Makas,

1988; Zahn, 1973). A key issue is how people who do not have disabilities treat those who do. People who do not have disabilities and persons with disabilities tend to have different conceptions about the proper ways to act regarding disability, which can increase social discomfort (Makas, 1988). A person with a disability may be offended if someone he or she does not know offers to help with some task, while the person offering the help may have the best of intentions and not understand why the person with a disability is upset. To the person with a disability, the offer of help may be seen as disempowering, while the rejection of the well-meaning offer may strike the other person as ungrateful or bitter. In this situation, each person did not really understand how best to deal with the other, creating social discomfort.

Social reactions to disability also frequently involve pity. Many people assume that an individual with a disability is in a perpetual state of mourning for what he or she cannot do as a result of the disability (Vash & Crewe, 2004). The person with the disability is reduced by such reactions to an object of sympathy who is seen as unable to be a meaningful participant in society or to lead a fulfilling life (Swain, French, & Cameron, 2003). Pity "makes disability salient and defining" by placing a person with a disability in "a position of presumed need" (Makas, 1988, p. 50). People who acquire disabilities during the course of their lives, rather than being born with disabilities, seem to be particular foci for pity. They are often pitied specifically because they are perceived as suffering "feelings of loss from which they will have no gain and from which they will never completely recover" (Swain et al., 2003, p. 68). Efforts by persons with disabilities to reassure others that they may be perfectly content in spite of having a disability, curiously enough, are often to no avail (Linton, 1998b).

Turning a person with a disability into a hero is another common social reaction. This reaction is interesting—on the surface it appears to be positive, but it is actually a different type of negative reaction. The hero reaction usually appears in the form of a compliment like, "I find you so inspiring" or "I am amazed that you can do that" or something similar. These comments, though they show comprehension of the impacts of a disability, also serve to distance the person with a disability from the speaker. A disability is always there and living with it is not a heroic act. It is simply one way of living. To make a person with a disability a hero or an inspiration serves to distance the person with the disability from "normal" people. This is evidenced by the fact that people who view persons with disabilities as heroes may not accept any views that contradict this position, even when expressed by persons with disabilities (Vash & Crewe, 2004). Being viewed as a hero may be better than being viewed as a defective wretch, but both perceptions marginalize the persons in question and make them into outsiders.

"You are such an inspiration." I could have cried. Why was I constantly being told I was an inspiration when all I was doing was my job? Because I smiled?

Because I was successful? Colleagues across the country were doing similar work; the only difference was that I had a disability. It is discomforting to know that you are not expected to succeed if you have a disability. Where did this notion come from? Why is it still so prevalent?

Discounting the importance of a disability in a person's life also serves to marginalize persons with disabilities. As a social reaction, dismissing the impact of disability is not uncommon. People generally do not accept that the social exclusion of individuals with disabilities is comparable to social exclusion based on race, gender, religion, or national origin (Francis & Silvers, 2000). Yet the social deprivations and scourges inflicted on persons with disabilities certainly are no less significant than those that have affected these other populations. Persons with disabilities are "subject to prejudiced attitudes, discriminatory behavior, and institutional and legal constraints that parallel" those faced by other minority populations (Scotch & Schriner, 1997, p. 149). In fact, the historical discussions in the next two chapters reveal that persons with disabilities have faced a tremendous amount of socially imposed suffering in virtually every culture around the world throughout human history.

Constructing social meaning for disability can be very difficult even for people with disabilities. The social classifications of disability by others can cause a great deal of self-consciousness or confusion in people with disabilities. One author mused about what it meant to come to social terms with his disability: "Celebrate it in song? Drink toasts to it in the bar? Talk endlessly about tragedy? Decry a poor quality of life? Limp bravely into the sunset giving inspiration to all other people?" (Pfeiffer, 2000, p. 98).

Some people with disabilities even try to avoid spending time with or being associated with other people with disabilities and can even be guilty of stereotyping other people with disabilities (Thomson, 1997). Persons with disabilities who are able to reject the negative social reactions of others still face dilemmas, such as being left to wonder about the cause of all the negative social reactions that they must perpetually struggle against. The people who most intimately know disability can at times have difficulty handling it as a social issue, due both to the reactions of others and to the very personal nature of disability.

Ultimately, social classifications of disability create the basis for social reactions to disability by establishing accepted perceptions about the roles and capabilities of persons with disabilities. To better understand how the social classifications and common social reactions to disability have developed, the history of the treatment of individuals with disabilities must be examined. By doing so, the development of social classifications of and reactions to disability will become clearer, as will the progression of how these classifications and reactions have been applied to create the present position of disability in society.

3

Disability Discrimination and the Evolution of Civil Rights in Democratic Societies

The worldwide population of individuals with disabilities is estimated to be as high as 550 million people (Albrecht & Verbugge, 2000; Metts, 2000). However, the practice of legally defined civil rights for individuals with disabilities is a very new concept, barely a quarter of a century old. Even in nations where legally defined civil rights have developed, disability remains at the periphery of society, as the new legal rights have yet to break established social classifications. This history demonstrates how negative social classifications of and reactions to persons with disabilities influenced the way in which they were treated by societies. This chapter reveals the length and depth of the struggle for basic acceptance and inclusion by individuals with disabilities. For most of this history, social reactions and classifications led to negative legal classifications and social exclusion. These social conditions have progressed from complete exclusion to a recent turn toward inclusion in many societies.

To understand the magnitude of the struggle for rights for individuals with disabilities in society, familiarity with the social and political history of these individuals is vital. Discrimination against individuals with disabilities is not unique, as many other groups face institutionalized discrimination in society. However, individuals with disabilities have faced particularly harsh treatment throughout history and have gone unacknowledged for a longer period of time than most other disenfranchised groups. The history of the treatment of individuals with disabilities is exceptionally unpleasant, to put it mildly. Few rights were established for individuals with disabilities in any nation or society until well into the twentieth century. In many places, individuals with disabilities still lack basic legal rights, much less access to education, health care, information technology, or the political process. Understanding the history related to disability is essential to understanding disability in modern society.

DISABILITY IN SOCIETY BEFORE THE NINETEENTH CENTURY

For much of human history, the idea of providing legal rights to individuals with disabilities was never even considered. From ancient times to the not-so-distant past, disability was often classified as a manifestation of the anger of a deity or supernatural power (Rosen, 1968). "Conspicuously abnormal persons were surrounded by superstition, myth, and fatalism—especially fatalism" (Winzer, 1997, p. 76). In many societies, the birth of an individual with a disability was viewed as a prophetic sign of impending doom (Warkany, 1959). Not surprisingly considering these attitudes, the inclusion of individuals with disabilities in the mainstream of society did not receive attention in most places until recent years.

Archaeologists have discovered the existence of disability dating back thousands of years in remains found in North America, South America, Europe, the Middle East, and Asia (Albrecht, 1992). Some people even had early forms of assistive technologies. Wooden prostheses were mentioned in writing in approximately 500 BCE, while a tomb from about 300 BCE was found to contain a skeleton with a bronze prosthetic leg (Braddock & Parish, 2001).

At the height of civilization in ancient Greece and Rome, what is now considered humankind's classical period, disability was kept "all but invisible, save a few blind prophets" (Edwards, 1997, p. 29). It was socially acceptable to abandon babies born with disabilities on sunny hillsides, tied or staked down, so as to perish from exposure to the sun (Garland, 1995). The law of the Greek state of Sparta, at the peak of its power, actually mandated the killing of children with disabilities, leaving the family no choice in the matter (Garland, 1995; Stiker, 1999). The fate of those who escaped death could still be most unhappy. For example, Balbous Balaesus the Stutterer, a Roman citizen, was kept in a cage along the main road to Rome so travelers could be amused by his speech problems when he tried to communicate with passersby (Garland, 1995). Blind boys in Rome were often trained as beggars, while blind girls were frequently sold into prostitution (French, 1932). Wealthy Roman households sometimes purchased individuals with disabilities to serve as amusement (Kanner, 1964). A special market even existed for the sale of these persons (Durant, 1944). Similarly, Egyptian pharaohs kept persons with disabilities both to provide entertainment and to bring good luck (Braddock & Parish, 2001).

This practice of using individuals with mental impairments as comic slaves was also common in ancient China and in pre-Columbian American civilizations (Willeford, 1969). Ancient Chinese culture, nearly 2,000 years ago, created a term to describe individuals with disabilities that translates to "disabled person, good for nothing," demonstrating an "all-too prevalent hostility and disregard for disabled people in China" (Stone, 1999, p. 137). That term is still commonly used to describe individuals with disabilities in China, and it has only started to be replaced by the slightly less derogatory term, "disabled but not useless," in recent years (Stone, 1999, p. 136). Chinese is hardly the only language that has this feature, as languages from Brazil to Zimbabwe use terms for disability that describe the person with a disability as "useless" or "afflicted as punishment" or "helpless" or "someone without freedom" (Charlton, 1998).

Worldwide, the situation really did not improve much until the recent past, as the mistreatment, abuse, neglect, and abandonment of individuals with disabilities has been commonplace throughout thousands and thousands of years of human history. Individuals with disabilities have been locked away against their will in prisons, asylums, and monasteries; they have been considered witches; and they have been thought to be suffering demonic possession. Often, forced confinement removed individuals with disabilities from any interaction with society whatsoever. Individuals with disabilities have often provoked "a kind of panic both internal and public" that has resulted in oppression, exclusion, and banishment to wretched institutions (Stiker, 1999, p. 9). That panic resulted in individuals with disabilities throughout history being killed, exiled, neglected, shunned, used for entertainment, or even treated as spiritual manifestations, both good and evil (Bragg, 1997; Hewett, 1974).

Much of the foundation for discrimination against persons with disabilities, particularly in Europe and the Americas, can actually be traced to early religious traditions and the foundations of modern religions. For many centuries, organized religions tended to express contradictory attitudes toward disabilities, with conflicting views of whether persons with disabilities should be shunned, punished, eradicated, or aided all being supported by major religious texts and leaders (Braddock & Parish, 2001; Winzer, 1997). Both the Old Testament and the New Testament of the Bible, for example, tend to equate disability with divine punishment or evidence of immoral behavior (Eisenberg, 1982; Shapiro, 1993). In the Old Testament, physical disability reflects spiritual disfavor as a result of sin, while in the New Testament persons with disabilities are viewed as possessed by evil or cursed (Shapiro, 1993). In the New Testament, the disciples even evidence the belief that disability was caused by sin, and this attitude "may be indicative of prevailing wisdom" of the time (Braddock & Parish, 2001, p. 17). These views are still reflected in many modern faiths (Shapiro, 1993). For religions that believe in reincarnation, such as Hinduism, disability poses a unique problem, as such religions typically believe that a person has a disability as punishment for something done in a previous life (Charlton, 1998). To that way of thinking, a disability always negatively reflects on the individual with a disability.

Beyond the parameters of religion, these religious views have had a tremendous social impact on the ways that persons with disabilities have been viewed and treated throughout history into the present day. "By associating sin and moral transgression with the resultant 'just retribution' of disability and illness, our society has found an apparent justification for stigmatizing the disabled" (Eisenberg, 1982, p. 5). These views have permeated many social and legal classifications of persons with disabilities.

Until the twentieth century, legal classifications of persons with disabilities were almost invariably negative. "The unwritten law of primitive society that the crippled and the disabled were to be sacrificed for the good of the group was carried over into written laws" (Funk, 1987, p. 9). Based on the Torah, Hebraic law created some classifications of individuals with disabilities (Stiker, 1999). However, "[l]egal uncleanness was attached to the disabled," denying them many social rights, leading to exclusion or denunciation in many cases (Stiker, 1999, p. 24). Persons with hearing impairments were particularly vulnerable under biblically based laws and societies, as the Old Testament describes faith as coming through hearing, leaving individuals with hearing impairments without faith in the view of many, including the early Christian church (Daniels, 1997). Further, as Christianity, over time, became "the religion of the written revelation" with strong ties between faith and visual imagery (De Hamel, 1994, p. 11), the visually impaired were unable to participate in what was for a long time considered another key part of that faith.

Jurists interpreting Greek and Roman law were primarily concerned with disability as a cause of actions in legal cases; for example, Roman law allowed for the appointment of guardians for individuals with mental illnesses (Gaw, 1906, 1907). One curious feature of Roman law is that deaf persons who could communicate verbally had the right to be citizens, while those who could not communicate verbally did not have the right to be citizens (Gaw, 1906). The Code of Justinian, compiled beginning in 533 CE under orders of the Roman Emperor Justinian, created a unified code of civil law for the empire that had a tremendous impact on the laws of most of Europe until well into the eighteenth century. This code and companion digests of Roman case law detailed many legal rights that individuals with certain types of disability, particularly individuals with mental, visual, or hearing impairments, were not allowed to have, such as the right to inherit property (Watson, 1998). As a result, the classification of persons with disabilities as lacking social, legal, or educational rights was institutionalized for well over a millennium under legal systems derived from or influenced by the Code of Justinian, which included virtually all of Europe.

Even in the supposedly more enlightened periods of human history, individuals with disabilities still faced unfortunate popular movements that emphasized institutionalization in poorhouses or worse, segregation, eugenics, sterilization, and forced relocation to colonies. "Being different drew cruel and callous reactions from society, yet the penalties inflicted—legal sanctions, church expulsion, starvation, exile, or even death—were too unevenly administered to exterminate all persons with disabilities" (Winzer, 1997, p. 80). In keeping with the Roman tradition, wealthy Italian households, including those of some popes, continued for centuries to own servants with disabilities as entertainment (Hibbert, 1975). In many different societies, individuals with disabilities also were used for public spectacle or sport, often with the risk of death to the unwilling participants (French, 1932). Prior to the eighteenth century, individuals with disabilities were usually allowed to interact with society only "under supervision" (Stiker, 1999, p. 69).

If their families would not support them, individuals with disabilities often were forced to beg to survive. Begging became so important to individuals with disabilities in the Middle Ages that guilds and brotherhoods of beggars with disabilities were created (Covey, 1998). As a result, "disability became synonymous with beggary, and beggary became synonymous with failure— failure to be wholly human because human worth was increasingly being associated with work" (Branson & Miller, 2002, p. 7). Individuals with certain impairments, such as mental disorders and epilepsy, were often locked away in asylums, madhouses, and prisons, while individuals with Hansen's disease (commonly known as leprosy) were forced to live in isolated camps, with Europe having as many as 19,000 leprosy villages at one time (Braddock & Parish, 2001; Foucault, 1965). Individuals with disabilities also were commonly exiled by being sent via boat to some other community (Foucault, 1965).

The anatomical and physiological studies of human anatomy during the Renaissance, performed by Leonardo da Vinci, Versalius, William Harvey, and others, led to better understandings of vision, hearing, and other systems of the body. Such advances, however, did not have a sizeable impact on the views of society toward persons with disabilities. During the Reformation, both John Calvin and Martin Luther advocated the classification of individuals with mental disabilities as creations of Satan (Braddock & Parish, 2001; Shorter, 2000). Luther actually favored praying for the death of individuals with cognitive disabilities or even killing them outright, as he believed that they were masses of flesh that lacked souls (Kanner, 1964; Shorter, 2000). In Renaissance times, it was common to beat individuals with cognitive disabilities on the head as a "treatment" (Braddock & Parish, 2001). From a bleakly ironic perspective, this treatment might be considered a profoundly misguided first attempt by a society to provide rehabilitative services to individuals with disabilities.

In colonial North America, the earliest known attempt to educate an individual with a disability occurred in 1679 when a tutor named Phillip Nelson began teaching a deaf child to communicate in a systematic manner (Fay, 1899). Nelson was forced to stop his work by the community in which he and his student lived because the local church denounced his work as blasphemy for attempting to perform a miracle and threatened Nelson's life (Fay, 1899). Thus, the people of North America have the curious legacy that they almost put their first special educator to death. This irrational opposition to educating individuals with disabilities was heavily influenced by the Puritan belief that a disability was unquestionably a manifestation of divine punishment (Covey, 1998). Increase Mather, an early president of Harvard University, and his son, Cotton Mather, who is most famous for his part in the accusations and claims of witchcraft in the seventeenth century that led to the Salem witch trials, helped to popularize the perception of disability as heavenly wrath (Covey, 1998; Winship, 1994). About the same time that Phillip Nelson's life was being threatened for trying to educate a child with a hearing impairment, Jan Amos Komensky was advocating to reform education in eastern Europe so that it was provided equally to all children, regardless of class, status, or ability (Salder, 1966). Komensky's views were not widely accepted; he repeatedly faced exile and ridicule throughout his lifetime for his opinions on education (Salder, 1966).

Fortunately, the situation for individuals with disabilities began to slowly improve in the 1700s in Europe. A method for teaching communication to deaf individuals developed by a Spanish monk named Pedro Ponce de Leon around 1510 came to be widely recognized in Spain and France (Daniels, 1997). These early methods of teaching sign language inspired a number of European educators and reformers to create residential schools for children with hearing impairments, and later children with visual impairments, offering the first systematized education for individuals with disabilities (Winzer, 1997). In 1752, Benjamin Franklin and Thomas Bond founded the first general hospital in colonial America offering care and rehabilitation for individuals with disabilities (Morton, 1897). The hospital represented almost immeasurable progress for individuals with disabilities, as it was the first institution in early America to use the health care technology of the time to provide help to individuals with disabilities. Franklin and his rehabilitative hospital, sadly, did not reflect the beliefs of Franklin's famous and influential compatriots, though America would eventually become the crux of the movement toward access, inclusion, and civil rights for individuals with disabilities.

DISCRIMINATION IN THE FORMATION OF A DEMOCRACY

When the framers of the U.S. government created the Declaration of Independence, they were espousing views based on the moral imperatives of equality for all. This vision of equality, however, did not include all residents of the newly formed nation. In 1776, the colonies were in a frenzy inspired by Thomas Paine's writings, especially *Common Sense*. Paine's vision of a truly free government included universal suffrage, universal education, and universal participation. Paine's egalitarian views, however, were considered unspeakably radical by many of the people who were establishing the U.S. government on principles of equality for certain parts of society. The Declaration was nevertheless intended "as a moral statement. Human equality, they were insisting, is a moral and even a religious standard against which it is right and proper to judge a political system" (Dahl, 2001, p. 124). The practicalities of the freedoms offered by the Declaration were not all-inclusive by any means. Though it stated that all men were created equal, all men were not to have equal rights of suffrage or participation in the new government, while women were excluded completely.

The U.S. constitutional government, as a representational republic, was unprecedented in human history. Representative governments had managed to exist and grow, such as the British Parliament and the Scandinavian Tings, but they were hardly republics, with great inequalities among the population and many other highly undemocratic features (Dahl, 2001). The modern parliamentary system did not yet exist and no large republic with popular representation had ever been attempted. The only successful republican governments in history were long-gone city-states of the classical era in the Mediterranean and the Middle Ages in southern Europe (Dahl, 1998). For all the innovation of the new republic, it did not create a wholly inclusive democracy.

Before, during, and after the Constitutional Convention, the rights of various groups were hotly contested issues. In the early history of the republic, the rights of women, slaves, Native Americans, immigrants, and the poor were widely discussed. Many of the founders, in fact, were publicly in favor of emancipation of all slaves and extending the right to vote to women and the poor (Kennedy, 2003; West, 1997). However, the framers who favored a more inclusive republic were forced to accept the undemocratic features in order for the Constitution to be ratified; "as practical men they made compromises" (Dahl, 2001, p. 38). Those favoring the most inclusive republic possible had to sacrifice many ideals to have any republic at all.

One scholar lists the undemocratic elements of the Constitution as including the acceptance of slavery, the denial of suffrage to women and minorities, the system for selecting the president, the selection of senators by state legislatures, equal representation in the Senate, and the extensive power of the judiciary (Dahl, 2001). Many of the undemocratic elements of the Constitution have been altered over the course of the nation's history, through legislation, jurisprudence, or violence, or a combination of those factors. A civil war and the Thirteenth, Fourteenth, and Fifteenth Amendments to the Constitution destroyed slavery. The Fourteenth Amendment has also served to eliminate discrimination against many other groups. The protections of the Fourteenth Amendment extend to national origin (*Korematsu v. United States*, 1944), race (*Brown v. Board of Education*, 1954), alienage (*Graham v. Richardson*, 1971), gender (*Craig v. Boren*, 1976), and illegitimacy (*Trible v. Gordon*, 1977). The Seventeenth Amendment took the power to select senators away from the state legislatures and gave it to the general populace. Women gained the right to vote by the Nineteenth Amendment. The Supreme Court, however, has refused to extend the protections of the Fourteenth Amendment to include persons with disabilities (*City of Cleburne v. City of Cleburne Living Center, Inc.*, 1985).

The framers of the Declaration of Independence and the Constitution primarily held to the then-common belief that individuals with disabilities had to be protected, as they "could not fend for themselves" (Bryan, 1996, p. 4). In the colonial period, individuals with disabilities were primarily relegated to dependence on family members or the community or were placed in poorhouses (Braddock & Parish, 2001). When a person with a disability had no family that could provide support, the common practice was to contract provision of care to the lowest bidder (Funk, 1987). Individuals with disabilities often were actually turned away from communities, either through banishment or being refused the right to enter a community (Braddock & Parish, 2001; Shapiro, 1993). At the time of the American Revolution, the various colonies' laws related to disability included statutes that mandated deporting persons with physical disabilities, classifying all persons with disabilities as indigent, and requiring all persons with disabilities to wear distinguishing symbols on their garments that showed their classification (Switzer, 2003).

There were scattered concerns of what might become of war casualties, such as veterans who were amputees or otherwise permanently injured. Throughout the history of the United States, "[d]uring a war and immediately thereafter, state, federal and local governments put forth every effort to meet the needs of the veteran with a disability and his family" (Bryan, 1996, p. 6). Starting with the American Revolution, these efforts were in the form of financial compensation for physical losses (Switzer, 2003). These concerns even led to the first two federal laws related to disability, passed in 1776 and 1798, that provided compensation and medical care for soldiers who incurred disabilities while in service (Albrecht, 1992). However, after every war, the interest in veterans with disabilities has been very "short-lived" (Bryan, 1996, p. 6). The late eighteenth century, though, did include the development of a very rudimentary pension system for some people with mental disabilities in the United States (Braddock & Parish, 2001).

In the United States, social advances for individuals with disabilities first began to be made in the 1800s. Although they lacked specific legal rights, some individuals with disabilities were beginning to gain basic entrance into society. The first private education for students with visual impairments was offered in 1812, and private schooling for individuals with hearing impairments began in 1817 (Shapiro, 1993). In the 1840s, the first treatise on the education of students with disabilities was published in the United States. Eduoard Seguin's (1846) *The Moral Treatment, Hygiene, and Education of*

Idiots and Other Backward Children, though featuring a title that seems brainless at this distance, actually broke ground in a very radical way by asserting that children with disabilities could be educated and were worth educating.

The creation of asylums to treat people with mental disabilities began in earnest in the mid-1840s, due in large part to the efforts of Dorothea Dix, who wrote and lectured about the pervasive mistreatment of persons with mental disabilities (Brown, 1998). Inventor Alexander Graham Bell, whose creations include the telephone, worked to popularize special education in the United States, as well as the use of the term *special education* (Winzer, 1993). Helen Keller gave disability a publicly identifiable face through her childhood accomplishments in the 1880s of learning to read, write, and speak despite being blind and deaf and not having the benefit of a trained special educator. After graduating from Radcliffe in 1904, Keller became an advocate for the rights of women, racial minorities, the poor, and, of course, persons with disabilities (Loewen, 1995). In 1905, the first special education training courses for teachers were offered in the United States (Smith, 2001).

These sporadic advances, however, were occurring in a climate where more powerful social forces still worked to oppress, marginalize, and eliminate individuals with disabilities. The tendency to separate people with disabilities from the rest of society led to the establishment of residential institutions outside of the community (Wolfsenberger, 1969), which shaped the social roles and classifications of individuals with disabilities for many years. In the nineteenth century, most children with disabilities, if provided any health care or education at all, were sent to separate residential institutions, which were nothing like the schools other students attended (Winzer, 1993). The residential schools were "warehouses where people were isolated from society" (Smith, 2001, p. 15). The individuals housed in these residential schools were "confined and isolated rather than aided toward independence" and sheltered from the world in which they were believed unable to survive (Bryan, 1996, p. 4). Overall, "[t]his socially sanctioned segregation reinforced negative societal attitudes toward human difference" (Braddock & Parish, 2001, p. 52). Into the nineteenth century, people with hearing, speech, and visual impairments were commonly assumed to have limited intellects (Pfeiffer, 1993).

Traveling "freak shows" that displayed persons with physical and mental disabilities were very popular attractions at fairs, circuses, and exhibits in the eighteenth and nineteenth centuries in Europe and North America (Bogdan, 1988; Thomson, 1997). The people used in these shows were frequently sold to the shows for life by their parents; the organizers of the shows would construct elaborate stories to exaggerate the differences of persons with disabilities (Bogdan, 1988; Thomson, 1997). These freak shows helped to institutionalize the belief in society that disability should be equated with deviance (Thomson, 1997).

THE AGE OF EUGENICS

In the mid-nineteenth century, British scientist Francis Galton popular-ized a movement known as *eugenics*, which was a term of Galton's own devising. Eugenics was based on the principle that only certain people had the right to perpetuate their genetic materials through reproduction and, therefore, reproduction should be regulated based on an individual's char-acteristics and endowments. These beliefs were built on the revolutionary work of Charles Darwin, who was Galton's cousin. Darwin's concept of the survival of the fittest in nature led some to transfer survival of the fittest to people, though Darwin was deeply opposed to such assertions (Branson & Miller, 2002; Gould, 1996). Nevertheless, Galton was inspired to become a veritable geyser of bad ideas in relation to human fitness, including trying to quantify the attractiveness of the breeding populations of women in the British Isles by city. He ranked London highest and Aberdeen lowest, for those of you who are wondering.

One of Galton's biographers has described his ideas related to eugenics thus: "Rarely in the history of science has a generalization been made on the basis of so little concrete evidence, so badly put, and so naively conceived" (Cowan, 1985, p. 9). Galton rarely read scientific works and owned a very small library of books that mostly appeared to have never been read (Cowan, 1985). Perversely, his efforts were taken quite seriously by the scientific community and the educated public, leading Galton's concept of eugenics to burgeon into a way of thinking about disability that has threatened the existence of persons with disabilities ever since. Eugenics has been aptly described as "a rationale for atrocities" (Gray, 1999, p. 84).

In a series of curiously popular books, such as 1869's *Hereditary Genius: An Inquiry into Its Laws and Consequences*, Galton wrote of the need to eliminate what he viewed as undesirable elements through "selection of a permanent breed" of humans like purebred dogs or horses (p. 1). Along with reinforcing the rampant racism and sexism of the day, Galton advocated raising the standards of humankind by weeding out the elements that he felt were unfit, specifically persons with disabilities. Other books Galton wrote that promoted the "science" of eugenics included *Inquiry into Human Faculty* (1883) and *Natural Inheritance* (1889). The clear purpose of eu-genics was to help along evolution by "reducing the number of individuals that natural selection will have to eliminate" (Levine, 2002, p. 118). Gal-ton's followers extended his ideas to some jaw-dropping proposals. One author, for example, advocated treating unfit people the same way unfit horses are treated in the book *The Right to be Well Born or Horse Breeding in its Relation to Eugenics* (Stokes, 1917).

These biased and unscientific theories became popular in the late nine-teenth and early twentieth centuries in many parts of the world under the influence of Europe. The ideas particularly took root in the United States, leading to many disturbing proposals by legislators and policymakers. Some of these upsetting ideas included placing all individuals with disabilities on islands by themselves (isolated by gender), permanently locking away all individuals with disabilities in institutions, or segregating them from the rest of society in an isolated part of a sparsely populated state (Jaeger & Bowman, 2002; Winzer, 1993). Industrialist Andrew Carnegie funded a laboratory for the study of eugenics (Ridley, 1999). In Britain, local eugenics societies were commonplace by 1900 and the name Eugene was increasingly popular (Ridley, 1999). Marie Stopes, a pioneering advocate for birth control and women's rights in Britain, also embraced eugenics, calling for the sterilization of one third of the English male population, and disowned her own son for marrying a woman who wore glasses (Cohen, 1993; Vinen, 2000). Denmark, Norway, and Sweden soon after passed compulsory sterilization laws for persons with disabilities (Vinen, 2000). As a result of the eugenics movement, public perceptions soon associated disability with a range of degenerate and antisocial behaviors (Shorter, 2000).

The theory of eugenics led to some truly horrifying laws in the United States. In 1914, the University of Washington and a self-proclaimed Foundation for Child Welfare conducted a study of the laws of the 49 states, territories, and the District of Columbia concerning individuals with disabilities (Smith, Wilkinson, & Wagoner, 1914). The results are a parade of discrimination, brutal oppression, and dehumanization, though the authors make no comments about the upsetting nature of the laws, demonstrating the social approval for them. Of the 49 jurisdictions, 38 had laws prohibiting marriage for individuals with various types of disabilities, either completely or until the woman was past the age of reproduction, a violation of which would result in imprisonment in many cases (Smith et al., 1914). Twelve of the states had detailed laws dictating the "asexualization" of individuals with many types of disabilities (pp. 16–33). Most states had laws mandating the institutionalization or banishment of individuals with any one of a number of physical, emotional, and mental disabilities to euphemistically named "villages" (Smith et al., 1914). Around the same time, the first suggestions were made for the performance of lobotomies, the surgical destruction of a portion of the brain, on individuals with mental disabilities (Noll, 1995; Shorter, 2000). The United States was not the only country to establish these types of eugenics-based involuntary sterilization and segregation laws; Australia, Canada, and most nations of Europe did as well (Baker, 2002; Bulmer, 2003; Ridley, 1999; Vinen, 2000).

For many believers in eugenics, "feeble-mindedness" had to be combated through sterilization, regardless of whether the law provided legal permission. In these cases, feeble-mindedness was used as a catchall term to encompass most disabilities. The vasectomy was actually developed by a doctor in Indiana as a more efficient means of sterilizing males with disabilities; this doctor alone would ultimately perform 600 to 700 vasectomies on males with disabilities against their will (Burgdorf, 1980). Sterilization procedures were most likely to be performed on women and on the poor (Noll, 1995). In 1916 and 1917, one institution in Virginia performed hysterectomies on 80 patients with disabilities without any legal grounds for doing so (Noll, 1995). In many states that had sterilization laws, the laws have never been formally removed from the books or struck down by courts (Pfeiffer, 1999).

The sterilization of persons with disabilities was even memorialized through early films. In the 1920s, a motion picture titled *The Black Stork* dramatized the real-life crusade of one doctor who thought that children with disabilities should be "treated" with euthanasia rather than medical attention (Pernick, 1997). From 1922 to 1937, the U.S. Public Health Service released *The Science of Life*, a set of twelve filmstrips for use in high school biology classes that equated disability to many forms of death and ugliness, including seriously ill livestock, and promoted the notion of the elimination of persons with disabilities (Pernick, 1997). Eugenics, however, did have a few prominent critics, like legal crusader Clarence Darrow and journalist Walter Lippmann, who actively campaigned against eugenics laws and policies (Richards, 1987).

For states that legally sanctioned sterilization, it was commonly viewed as very important work. A North Carolina state official asserted in a medical journal article that sterilization was "an extremely important part of any well-rounded program for combating the problems of mental deficiency and disease" (Lawrence, 1947, p. 24). Sterilization was accomplished through many different means, including removal of reproductive organs, blasting areas of the body with tremendously high levels of X-ray radiation, or directly injecting the reproductive organs with radium (Noll, 1995; Proctor, 2002). Obviously, the negative health consequences often extended far beyond infertility. Many victims of these sterilization procedures were not even told what had been done to them (Gould, 1996). The Supreme Court of the United States upheld the legality of these practices so that the United States would not be "swamped with incompetence" and to "prevent those who are manifestly unfit from continuing their kind" (*Buck v. Bell*, 1927, p. 207).

The eugenics-based assault on persons with disabilities represents perhaps the most concerted attempt in history to eradicate disability from society, most notably in Nazi Germany. The Nazis persecuted and wantonly killed members of many groups—Jews, political dissidents, intellectuals, gypsies, gays, Jehovah's Witnesses, Poles, Slavs, and many others. Persons with disabilities, in particular, were targeted by the Nazi regime for utter annihilation. In 1933, shortly after the Nazis assumed power, they passed a law designed to forcibly sterilize persons with a range of disabilities. The text of this law was, sadly, heavily influenced by the eugenics laws of California (Reilly, 1991). The German law was extremely thorough, mandating the sterilization of people with mental disabilities, mental illnesses, epilepsy, deafness, blindness, physical deformities, and alcoholism, among other conditions (Friedlander, 1995, 1999). In 1934, 181 Hereditary Health Courts were established to deliberate cases of whether specific individuals should be sterilized under the law, while in the same year the German Medical Association established a scholarly journal devoted to issues of who should be sterilized (Friedlander, 2002). In 1935, a subsequent law prevented persons with disabilities from marrying (Friedlander, 1995, 1999). These laws basically removed persons with disabilities from most social roles.

The sterilization laws created a new scientific and medical field in Germany, with manufacturers working to create new sterilization tools and 180 medical student dissertations being devoted to advances in sterilization (Proctor, 2002). These laws led to the sterilization of over 375,000 to 400,000 persons with disabilities in Germany alone (Friedlander, 2002; Reilly, 1991). The sterilization efforts of Germany in the 1930s did not go unnoticed in the United States, with officials of some states publicly lauding Germany's efforts (Noll, 1995).

The Nazi killing spree of persons with disabilities actually began in 1939, starting with children and infants with disabilities (Biesold, 1999). These activities, known as the T4 program, quickly came to include the murder of adults with disabilities in hospitals, sanitariums, institutions, schools, prisons, and concentration camps in Germany and all occupied territories (Biesold, 1999). Physicians and scientists harvested the internal organs of many of the victims for research (Friedlander, 2002; Proctor, 2002). The families of those put to death were informed by letter that their loved ones had died from a brief, highly contagious illness that necessitated that the bodies be immediately cremated and their effects destroyed (Biesold, 1999; Friedlander, 1999). The T4 program resulted in the forced abortions of uncounted fetuses and the slaughter of hundreds of thousands of children and adults with disabilities by means of starvation, lethal injections, the gas chamber, and overdoses of medication (Friedlander, 1995, 1999; Reilly, 1991).

In the mid to late 1930s, international support for sterilization began to wane. New scientific advances in biology, medicine, and other natural sciences began to undermine the principles of eugenics (Heberer, 2002). Sterilization and other eugenics-based "treatments" still had many proponents in the international scientific community, though. In 1935, a Nobel laureate argued for euthanasia for criminals and the mentally ill in a popular book, and the first lobotomy was performed (Proctor, 2002). In 1942, the *Journal of the American Psychiatric Association* published an article that argued for the killing of children with mental disabilities (Kennedy, 1942). Most of the remaining international support for eugenic theories, however, was obliterated by the revelations of Nazi war crimes (Friedlander, 2002).

California, Virginia, and North Carolina would ultimately perform the most forced sterilizations of persons with disabilities in the United States (Noll, 1995). Tens upon tens of thousands of sterilization procedures were performed between the mid-1800s and the 1970s in the United States

(Pfeiffer, 1999). Involuntary eugenic sterilizations also continued to occur in Canada, Sweden, and Scandinavia into the 1970s (Gillham, 2001). To this day, China continues to perform involuntary sterilizations of persons with certain disabilities (Bulmer, 2003). Ultimately, the greatest horror of eugenics may be rooted in the fact that it used the full compulsive power of the state to completely rob persons with disabilities of the fundamental sanctity of their own bodies. Eugenics clearly demonstrates the far-reaching consequences of negative classifications of disability.

CIVIL RIGHTS FOR INDIVIDUALS WITH DISABILITIES

The rise of industrialization did finally serve to create a sustained social awareness of disability and related issues in the early twentieth century. Industrial accidents and occupational hazards began to make physical disability a growing social concern. In the early 1900s, more than 500,000 members of the working-age population in the United States had a physical disability as a result of their work, with an average of 14,000 more workers joining those ranks each year (Zola, 1994). The trade union movement and workers' rights groups began to push for compensation for workers who suffered disabling injuries on the job; by 1920, almost every state in the United States had some form of compensation legislation (Zola, 1994). World War I created further attention to physical disability, as more than 123,000 Americans returned home with a physical disability (Gritzer & Arluke, 1985). In European nations, the numbers of persons with disabilities from the war were much greater. Germany, for example, was providing pensions for more than 750,000 veterans with war-related disabilities ten years after the end of the war (Vinen, 2000). This move to help veterans with disabilities, however, was not focused on integrating those with disabilities into society through education and health services, but rather compensating them for their lost wages and working potential (Frey, 1984). The respect for veterans with disabilities after World War I was socially limited, as well. A prominent British war hero with a combat related disability, Siegfried Sassoon, was forcibly confined to a mental institution after issuing a philosophical tract decrying the irrationality of war (Vinen, 2000).

Occasional disability rights protests did occur in the early twentieth century, such as a 1935 protest against disability discrimination by Depression-era work-relief programs (Longmore, 2003). The issue of disability was certainly becoming more pronounced in United States society by the 1950s. Medical advances allowed many soldiers to survive World War II who would have previously died from their injuries, helped many people recover from polio, and increased survival rates for many other illnesses and injuries (Barnartt & Scotch, 2001). The end result was an increase in the number of people in the population who had some kind of disability, as people who would have previously died from many maladies now survived with a disability (Barnartt & Scotch, 2001).

Individuals with disabilities, however, continued to be socially classified as irrelevant for most of the twentieth century. For example, in the early twentieth century, some parents still were selling their children with disabilities to side-shows, freak shows, and circuses (Switzer, 2003). Randolph Bourne, a disciple of John Dewey, who had severe physical disabilities, was writing and arguing in the early part of the twentieth century that America should lead the world in working to transcend cultural identity (Menand, 2001). Though his work discussed racial and ethnic characteristics, it is worth considering the impact of his disability on his desire to overcome social classifications. Individuals with disabilities clearly were saddled with undesirable and unfortunate social clas-sifications until the late twentieth century.

The presence of defined legal rights can be very powerful as a social classifi-cation by creating protections under the law and as a social symbol by ac-knowledging the importance of including a specific group of people. For per-sons with disabilities, the quest for legal rights was a quest to fulfill the goals of legal protection and social acknowledgment. Through the 1960s, the twentieth century had evidenced an increasing humanization in society of some persons with disabilities. However, social actions and attitudes reinforced the perception of persons with disabilities as "dependent, unhealthy deviants, who would, in the great majority, always require segregated care and protection" (Funk, 1987, p. 14).

Inspired by the civil rights movements for racial and gender equality of the 1950s and 1960s, persons with disabilities became very active in battling for legal rights in the early 1970s. The roots of the disability rights movement developed from many social and legal changes of the 1960s. In 1962, the family of President Kennedy began to publicly address issues of disability, including the fact that the president's sister had a disability (Shorter, 2000). This act began to remove some of the social stigma associated with dis-cussing issues of disability (Shorter, 2000). Returning Vietnam veterans with disabilities provided prevalent public faces for disability, while the passage of civil rights statutes for other segments of the public spurred organization and feelings of identification between persons with disabilities (Barnartt & Scotch, 2001).

In 1971, a court held for the first time that students with disabilities had a constitutional right to receive a public education. In *Pennsylvania Association for Retarded Children (PARC) v. Commonwealth of Pennsylvania* (1971), a federal district court held that the exclusion of children with disabilities from public school was unconstitutional. Since the state had the expressed goal of providing a free public education to all the children in the state, Pennsylvania could not deny students with disabilities access to free public education. The ground breaking *PARC* ruling immediately inspired disability rights groups in 36 other states to file suits against their state governments (Spring, 1993).

In 1973, the federal government passed the first law to grant specific, affirmative legal rights to individuals with disabilities—Section 504 of the

Rehabilitation Act. Section 504 was different from any previous laws that addressed disability, as it established "full social participation as a civil right" and represented a "transformation" of the legal rights of individuals with disabilities (Scotch, 2001, p. 3). The requirement that recipients of federal funds were barred from discriminating against individuals with disabilities was based on the requirements of the Civil Rights Act, which prohibited recipients of federal funds from discriminating based on race, color, or national origin. Also like the Civil Rights Act, Section 504 was intended to prevent both intentional and unintentional discrimination.

In 1973, President Nixon signed the Rehabilitation Act into law and then did absolutely nothing to implement or enforce the law. For the law to be effective, regulations and guidelines regarding requirements and enforcement had to be created by the Department of Health, Education, and Welfare (Bowe, 1979; Fleischer & Zames, 2001; Jaeger & Bowman, 2002; Scotch, 2001). After Section 504 was passed, legal scholars were still writing articles that legitimately spoke of a lack of federal government protections of persons with disabilities to receive even a minimal education (Handel, 1975; McClung, 1974; Stick, 1976). A 1976 lawsuit against the government began the chain of events that would lead to the enforcement of Section 504; in its holding, the court noted that Section 504 was not likely to implement or enforce itself (*Cherry v. Matthews*, 1976). Even a court order, however, did not get the Ford administration to start work on guidelines for Section 504; on the day the court order was issued, the executive branch immediately tried to send the matter back to Congress (Fleischer & Zames, 2001).

The problem was left for the Carter administration to address, an administration that continued to avoid the issue after taking office. These further delays spurred a series of protests by disability rights activists, including wheelchair blockades of certain government offices and of the home driveway of the Secretary of Health, Education, and Welfare, who had been threatening to issue guidelines that removed most of the power of the law (Fleischer & Zames, 2001; Shapiro, 1993). The government had also been holding closed-door meetings about the guidelines with a review committee that had no representation of disability organizations or members with disabilities (Longmore, 2003).

The protest in the San Francisco office of the Department of Health, Education, and Welfare lasted the longest, with 60 individuals with numerous types of disabilities staying 25 days and leaving only after the Section 504 regulations had been signed (Shapiro, 1993). The events that occurred during the demonstrations emphasized the bias that the protestors were fighting against. The government officials decided that the demonstrators should receive no food and should not be allowed communication outside the offices at each of the protests, while the Health, Education, and Welfare officials treated the demonstrators as misbehaving children, offering punch and cookies as a bribe to leave (Heumann, 1979; Shapiro, 1993). The demonstrators in San Francisco faced perhaps the most demeaning treatment, with a registered nurse being assigned to stay with the demonstrators to make sure they could look after themselves (Fleischer & Zames, 2001).

During their 25-day stay, the protestors in San Francisco gained national attention for the issue and received support from a wide range of people and organizations. United States Representatives Phillip Burton and George Miller ordered that food reach the demonstrators, and assistance flowed in from McDonald's, the California Department of Health Services, Safeway Markets, various unions, the Black Panthers, and San Francisco Mayor George Moscone, among others. A key event during the protests was a televised hearing held by Burton and Miller on the issue, to which the Department of Health, Education, and Welfare sent a low-ranking assistant to explain the delays (Longmore, 2003). The assistant reported that 22 major changes had to be made to the regulations before they would be promulgated, including the creation of exemptions to the requirements for accessibility features (such as ramps) for schools and hospitals, and the astounding change of not including students with disabilities in general education classrooms (Longmore, 2003). The impact of the protests, coupled with the increasingly untenable stance of the administration, finally forced the promulgation of the Section 504 guidelines. The first guidelines for Section 504, which did not dilute the impact of the law, finally were signed on April 28, 1977, and were formally issued on May 4, 1977.

The success of these protests also inspired subsequent disability rights protests. In the past 25 years, major disability rights protests have focused on issues related to education, funding for services, access to buildings, access to transportation, social attitudes and awareness, and laws and policies (Barnartt & Scotch, 2001). Over time, however, the social impact of these protests seems to be decreasing, as public, political, and media attention to disability rights protests has decreased even though the number of protests has increased (Barnartt & Scotch, 2001).

The efforts of the U.S. federal government since the belated implementation of Section 504 of the Rehabilitation Act have placed it at the forefront of articulating legal rights for persons with disabilities. In 1990, Congress passed a second extensive set of legal rights for individuals with disabilities, the Americans with Disabilities Act (ADA). Though a diverse group of organizations, politicians, and businesses lobbied against the passage of the ADA (Fleischer & Zames, 2001), the law passed easily, creating the most extensive set of legal rights for individuals with disabilities anywhere in the world. A large part of the reason for the strength of the ADA was the concerted and organized efforts by a range of disability rights and advocacy groups to ensure its success. When he signed the act, then President George H. W. Bush proclaimed, "Let the shameful wall of exclusion finally come tumbling down" (quoted in Shapiro, 1993, p. 140).

The ADA prohibits discrimination and requires equal opportunity in employment, state and local government services, public accommodations, commercial facilities, and transportation. Basically, the ADA extends the protections created by the Rehabilitation Act to most elements of society. The ADA prohibits discrimination against persons with disabilities by various private and public institutions, including state governments, and provides a mechanism for legal protection and remedies. The ADA instructs local and state governments that "no qualified individual with a disability shall...be excluded from participation in or be denied the benefits of the services, programs, or activities of a public entity" (42 U.S.C.A. § 12132). The Rehabilitation Act provides the same protections for federal agencies and any agency receiving federal assistance. The ADA has been determined to protect access to and use of such disparate public entities as universities (*Darian v. University of Massachusetts Boston*, 1987), courts (*People v. Caldwell*, 1995), and prisons (*Saunders v. Horn*, 1996). The ADA also prohibits discrimination by private organizations providing public accommodations, which traditionally has included hotels, restaurants, offices, housing, and shopping centers, among many others.

Since the passage of the ADA, the U.S. government has worked to continue to expand legal rights of access to new and developing technologies to individuals with disabilities. The Telecommunications Act of 1996 requires makers and providers of telecommunications equipment and services to ensure products can be used by persons with disabilities. Section 508 of the Rehabilitation Act, implemented in 2001, requires that citizens with disabilities, including federal employees, have equal access to and use of information and communication technologies used by the government. Section 508 establishes that the software applications, operating systems, Web-based information and applications, telecommunications products, video and multimedia products, self-contained or closed products, desktop computers, and portable computers of the government and organizations receiving federal funding must be accessible to individuals with disabilities. The requirements of Section 508 are extremely important to guaranteeing the delivery of technology-based information and services from the government in an equal manner for persons with disabilities.

However, despite the passage of disability rights laws and the increased role in parts of society for individuals with disabilities, there are many places where the laws clearly have not yet caused significant changes. For example, the ADA, though intended to dramatically increase the presence of individuals with disabilities in the workplace, has had limited success in this area, due to limited enforcement by the federal government and continuing lack of equal access to new information and communication technologies (Hignite, 2000; Kruse & Hale, 2003; Kruse & Schur, 2003; Lee, 2003; Wells, 2001). The Internet, as is discussed in detail in chapter 7, appears to be in danger of becoming another area where the laws are not having the desired impact.

In many professions, persons with disabilities are still a rarity. Individuals with disabilities have had to fight for an equal right to attend highly specialized professional programs, like medical school and law school, and to take professional licensing exams, like the medical boards or the bar exam. Given the continued scarcity of persons with disabilities in many fields, some lack of understanding and some outright bias are hardly unexpected. However, that occasional bias can be presented in some unique ways.

While in law school, Kevin, who had an obvious disability, was asked by one of the professors to come to his office for an important discussion. Kevin did not know this professor well, so he was curious about the reasons. At the professor's office, the professor said he needed to advise Kevin not to plan on practicing law as a career. After expressing that he was only being helpful, the professor explained that he felt persons with disabilities should not be lawyers because they would only be detrimental to their clients. The professor believed that persons with disabilities would not win many court cases because juries would not be sympathetic to a client who could only afford to hire "a defective." Anyway, someone with a disability would not have the capacity to work hard enough to be a successful lawyer. After the professor had finished, Kevin left his office and found himself less angry than amazed at the lengths people will go to try to disguise their own prejudices.

THE SUPREME COURT AND DISABILITY RIGHTS

The U.S. Supreme Court, unfortunately, has been curtailing the efforts of the Congress on behalf of individuals with disabilities for more than two decades. Since 1982, the Supreme Court has been acting to limit the rights of individuals with disabilities that Congress establishes. The basic theme throughout these cases is that the Supreme Court does not believe that persons with disabilities merit the same legal rights as other minority groups. The Supreme Court first tempered the Individuals with Disabilities Education Act in 1982 by holding that the law did not mandate that a student with a disability be provided the most effective form of assistance possible to improve his or her chance of receiving an equal education. Instead, the Supreme Court decided schools are only required to provide some educational assistance to make the educational environment more conducive to learning for the student. Three years later in *City of Cleburne v. City of Cleburne Living Center, Inc.* (1985), the Supreme Court addressed the rights of persons with disabilities to seek general legal protection as a group. The court concluded that disability did not merit the same level of constitutional protection as race, gender, national origin, and other group characteristics.

The Supreme Court's next major limitation of the rights of individuals with disabilities came in 1999 with a set of cases issued on the same day. *Albertsons, Inc. v. Kirkingburg* (1999), *Murphy v. United Parcel Service* (1999), and *Sutton v. United Air Lines, Inc.* (1999) established a new limitation on who qualifies for protection under disability laws. These cases created the standard that an individual can only qualify for legal protection under disability rights law if that individual is limited in a major life activity after the maximum corrections and mitigating measures are taken. For example, a person cannot be considered to have a disability under the ADA for having profound loss of eyesight if that sight problem can be corrected into the normal range through lenses or surgery. In *Sutton*, the court wrote: "Congress did not intend to bring under the protection of the ADA all those whose uncorrected conditions amount to disabilities" (p. 475). This set of cases places a burden on persons with disabilities to prove that they still have a disability in spite of whatever corrective measures might exist. If an individual has a profound loss that cannot be corrected into the normal range with any available measures, then that individual qualifies for protection under the law. The individual, however, may have to demonstrate that he or she has a disability no matter what corrective measures are taken.

In 2001, the Supreme Court significantly limited the scope of the ADA. In *Board of Trustees of the University of Alabama v. Garrett*, the Supreme Court modified the ADA with regard to employment actions by state governments. The court held that state governments were not liable to suit for monetary damages under the ADA for employment discrimination based on disability, but still could be forced to comply with the act. Though this may not sound like a large difference, the effect is sizeable. Instead of having to pay monetary damages for violating the employment rights of persons with disabilities, state governments now must only contend with being told to stop discriminating by the courts. Perhaps most disturbing is the fact that the majority opinion in this case treats the history of discrimination against persons with disabilities as if it was relatively innocuous and inconsequential, dismissing it as anecdotal and exaggerated.

In 2002, the court went a step further in chipping away at the rights of individuals with disabilities (National Council on Disability, 2003a, p. 2). In the holding of *Toyota v. Williams* (2002), the Supreme Court constricted the definitions of disability under the ADA, limiting the coverage of the law exclusively to people who met the strictest meanings of its definition of disability. While the definitions in all other types of civil rights laws are interpreted broadly, the court held that the ADA must be "interpreted strictly to create a demanding standard for qualifying as disabled" (pp. 197–198). In 2004, one Supreme Court opinion (*Tennessee v. Lane*) at least countered the trend of limiting the scope of the ADA by holding that the ADA did definitely guarantee equal access to the courts in the United States.

These decisions by the Supreme Court have evidenced a clear intent to limit disability rights laws as much as possible, though Congress, in passing the laws, meant them to be interpreted broadly (National Council on Disability, 2002). The decisions also have resulted in considerable bias in favor of the defendant in any discrimination claims under the ADA (Burgdorf, 1997; Colker, 1999; Feldblum, 2000; Tucker, 2000). A further result of these decisions has been a wave of lower federal court decisions that make it much more difficult for people to prove that they have a disability that substantially limits a major life activity, to establish that they have taken all the possible mitigating measures, to prove they have been discriminated against, and to show that they fall within the definition of disability (National Council on Disability, 2003b). Ultimately, the Supreme Court decisions have also had a chilling effect on claims brought under disability rights laws, significantly reducing the number of claims that are even filed because many persons with disabilities now assume the courts are biased against them (National Council on Disability, 2003b).

Some state governments are actively working to counter the holdings of the Supreme Court that limit who qualifies as having a disability. Though the majority of state governments have modified their state disability rights laws to mirror the Supreme Court limitations on the rights of individuals with disabilities, California, Connecticut, Massachusetts, New Jersey, New York, Rhode Island, Washington, and West Virginia have not. California and Rhode Island have actually amended their state laws to explicitly reject federal case law that limits who is protected by disability rights laws, while the Supreme Courts of Massachusetts and West Virginia have both recently rejected the U.S. Supreme Court holdings related to disability (National Council on Disability, 2003a).

DISABILITY AS A GROWING WORLDWIDE ISSUE

The worldwide population of persons with disabilities is estimated to be as many as 550 million, but only 15 percent of persons with disabilities have had a disability since birth (Albrecht & Verbugge, 2000; Metts, 2000). As such, disability is an emerging global issue that "will be on the rise for many decades to come, fueled by population aging, environmental factors, and social violence" (Albrecht & Verbugge, 2000, p. 305). The population of persons with disabilities is expected to rise in both technologically advanced nations and less developed nations (Priestley, 2001). Though social attitudes toward persons with disabilities have improved, individuals with disabilities are still very much a minority in status and social power the world over. "Disabled people are marginalized and excluded from mainstream society.... Disabled people definitely represent one of the poorest groups in Western society" (Kitchin, 1998, p. 343).

In many less developed nations, persons with disabilities literally are at the bottom of society, being described, without exaggeration, as "the poorest and most powerless people on earth" (Charlton, 1998, p. 25). In various less developed nations at this time, persons with disabilities often are deprived of education, abandoned, left in the care of inadequate state services, trained as beggars, prevented from marrying, sterilized, or even subject to infanticide or other forms of extermination (Charlton, 1998; Priestley, 2001). Persons with disabilities are so marginalized that in some societies they are treated as if they do not exist. In India, persons with disabilities are not included in the national census (Ghai, 2001). There are few greater denials of personhood than being informed that your existence is not relevant to the national census.

The nations that have created legal protections for individuals with disabilities remain in the minority (Metts, 2000). In spite of the still significant social barriers discussed in this chapter, individuals with disabilities may have more legally defined rights in the United States than anywhere else. The passage of Section 504 of the Rehabilitation Act, the Individuals with Disabilities Education Act, and the ADA place the United States in the vanguard of disability rights in the international community. Many nations, along with the United Nations, have developed laws, regulations, and policies that were inspired and influenced by the ADA. These nations have developed laws that take a range of approaches to disability rights (Blanck, Hill, Siegal, & Waterstone, 2003; Jones & Marks, 1999).

A plethora of nations, including Australia, Austria, Brazil, Denmark, Finland, Germany, Malawi, the Philippines, South Africa, Sweden, and Uganda, adopted laws or amended their constitutions in the 1990s to provide the first real legal rights for individuals with disabilities (Metts, 2000). Some emphasize defining who qualifies as having a disability, while others focus on reducing barriers to social inclusion as a result of disability (National Council on Disability, 2003a). Zimbabwe passed a law in 1992 prohibiting any social, cultural, or physical barriers to equal participation for individuals with disabilities. Australia passed a law in 1993 outlawing discrimination on the basis of specific disabilities. Venezuela adopted a law in 1994 that protects individuals with disabilities from being socially excluded as a result of a disability. In 1995, the United Kingdom passed its disability rights law, which is deeply indebted to, but not nearly as far-reaching as, the ADA. While the law does establish basic legal rights for individuals with disabilities in the United Kingdom, it has been criticized for being too limited (Doyle, 1996, 1997; Gooding, 1996). Though the legal rights established by these laws vary greatly, each represents a step forward in the effort to gain and preserve equal rights for individuals with disabilities around the world.

The United Nations (1994) has adopted the *Standard Rules on the Equalization of Opportunities for Persons with Disabilities*. These rules, which have no force of law, established basic standards that nations were encouraged to adopt to provide equal opportunities to individuals with disabilities, including rights to equal participation and rights to education and rehabilitation. The rules were partially based on an early United Nations (1982) declaration called the *World Programme of Action Concerning Disabled Persons* that argued for taking preventative actions to limit future cases of disability (such as improved health care, better diet, and limiting armed conflicts) and increasing participation in society for individuals with disabilities. The European Union (1996) has also adopted general disability guidelines that are intended to function as rules for European Union activities and basic guides for the laws of all member nations. The European Community, the predecessor of the European Union, first formally acknowledged the need for the guarantee of legal rights for persons with disabilities in 1986 (Daunt, 1991). The European Union even declared 2003 to be the Year of the Disabled in the European Union, though the accompanying activities seemed primarily designed to promote awareness of what was already happening in the nations of Europe rather than pressing for positive change in the social treatment or civil rights of individuals with disabilities.

These changes in attitudes toward persons with disabilities, however, are far from widely accepted in many parts of the world. Evidence of ingrained social classifications that are not changing can be found in the language used to describe persons with disabilities. In many regions of the world, socially accepted terms still used to identify persons with disabilities translate into useless, helpless, deserving punishment, inability to do anything for oneself, and many other terms that serve to marginalize and disempower (Charlton, 1998).

This chapter has traced the relationships between social reactions and classifications, legal classifications, and the social position of persons with disabilities. For most of this history, negative social reactions and classifications led to negative legal classifications and social exclusion. The changes in recent history demonstrate the progress that has been made by persons with disabilities toward social inclusion. This progress, however, is far from complete. Persons with disabilities still face considerable discrimination in innumerable ways in their daily lives. Even today, society often tends to encourage family members to view someone with a disability as a dependent and, in certain ways, even encourages people with disabilities to act as dependents (Pfeiffer, 2000; Ware, 2002).

Discrimination against disability can even extend to the right to enter a country. Chapter 4 traces the role disability discrimination has played in immigration into the United States. It traces the changes in social classifications of, legal classifications of, and reactions to disability over time in this area. The chapter also demonstrates how negative classifications of and reactions to individuals with disabilities have been used as an excuse to discriminate against other groups as well.

4

Trying to Come to America:
A Historical Illustration of
the Classifications of Disability
in U.S. Immigration Law and Policy

The evolution of the treatment of disability in immigration illustrates the development of social and legal classifications of and reactions to disability throughout history in the United States. This chapter examines the history of how the classification of disability has been applied to limit entrance to the United States by certain groups, who either had a disability or who were deemed socially undesirable for reasons other than disability. The social attitudes toward, and laws related to, immigration demonstrate the complex interactions of social reactions, social classifications, legal classifications, and the social status and rights of persons with disabilities. Immigration policy is one of numerous potential examples of the interrelationship of these issues; it is used here because of how well it highlights the life-altering impacts of reactions to and classifications of disability. Though some policies described in this chapter are no longer in place, many lasted through the 1980s and 1990s, while a few are still enforced.

As noted in chapter 3, individuals with disabilities in colonial America were frequently forced out of towns and were often forcibly sent back to Europe (Shapiro, 1993). Once the colonies evolved into the United States, people with disabilities who wished to come to America were still subjected to discriminatory immigration policies. In fact, the purported or assumed presence of a disability was often used as an excuse to exclude other groups who were deemed socially undesirable even when disability was not present. For much of its history, the United States officially limited entrance into the nation based on physical and mental disabilities. In fact, "the exclusion of disabled people was central to the laws and the work of the immigration service" for much of its history (Baynton, 2001, p. 47). These policies were described both as attempts to prevent furtherance of hereditary and contagious conditions and as ways to prevent the creation of an entire class of economic dependents (Johnson, 2004; *United States v. Tod*, 1923). However, based on the available historical record of legal and government documents, many individuals with disabilities that were not allowed to immigrate clearly neither had a contagious disease nor were likely to become wards of the state. The policies of inadmissibility for health reasons appear to have often had a very insidious use in practice, namely discrimination against individuals with disabilities and other groups that have been deemed undesirable as immigrants at various times in the history of the nation.

The exclusion of potential immigrants due to their disabilities also sent an incredibly strong message to native-born persons with disabilities. Without the sheer luck of being born in the United States, they would never have had a chance of living here. If someone with a disability was not good enough to become a U.S. citizen, the same policy sent a clear message that U.S. citizens with disabilities were a lower class of citizen or were not worthy of being citizens at all.

The Office of the Attorney General and the judicial branch of the U.S. government have historically given the greatest discretion possible to immigration officials in making admissibility decisions (*Alvarez v. District Director of U.S. Immigration and Naturalization Service*, 1976; *Dunn v. I.N.S.*, 1974; *Noel v. Chapman*, 1975). As a result, in many cases where an immigrant or a refugee was denied entrance to the United States and the official reason was inadmissibility due to health concerns, the decisions were given deference. Though surely many aliens from groups that were socially unpopular at the time were denied entrance for legitimate reasons, many immigrants appear to have been deemed inadmissible for purely discriminatory reasons. For example, during a certain period of time when there was a strong national bias against Asians, immigrants from Asia were often deemed inadmissible for reasons of health concerns, though, upon inspection, some of these cases seem questionable.

Courts have stated that an immigration regulation showing "invidious discrimination" is unconstitutional (*Faustino v. Immigration and Naturalization Service*, 1969). However, a review of the history of nonadmission of immigrants and refugees for health reasons reveals an undercurrent of using the policy to keep out those who were seen as social undesirables. Depending on the era, these undesirables have included people with physical or mental disabilities that neither were contagious nor rendered them helpless, immigrants from specific nations, and homosexuals. In the cases of immigrants from specific nations and immigrants suspected of being homosexual, the supposed presence or the potential threat of disability was used as reason to prevent these people from immigrating. However, in all of these cases, the feared or purported presence of disability was the ultimate way to keep out social undesirables, demonstrating that disability was seen as the most undesirable characteristic of all.

THE EXCLUSION OF ALIENS BASED ON PHYSICAL OR MENTAL DISABILITY

As a diverse and multicultural nation, the United States tends to celebrate its origins in "doughty wayfarers, the country they made, and the country they hoped to find" (Yans-McLaughlin, 1990, p. 4). The Unites States is a nation composed primarily of immigrants and their descendants, but beginning in the mid-nineteenth century, many citizens of the United States publicly espoused the view that immigration should be limited. These schemes for limiting admission to the country hinged on disablism, racism, classism, and other forms of intolerance. Denial of entrance to a certain nationality, socioeconomic class, religious group, or race was often part of a statement that admission to the United States should be limited. This rhetoric hardly changed over the course of a 150-year period.

In the 1890s, one of the best-selling books was *The Passing of the Great Race*, which claimed that scientific studies had shown that unrestricted immigration would lead to the degeneration of the nation (Tsai, 1983). Other popular titles on immigration of the time included books with subtle titles like *The Unwelcome Immigrant, Bitter Strength*, and *The Indispensable Enemy* (Tsai, 1983). Even Woodrow Wilson's (1902) *History of the American People* claimed recent immigration was ruining the country by admitting people from lower economic classes in eastern Europe and advanced the rather undemocratic suggestion that Asian immigrants should be admitted to the nation exclusively as minimal workers, with minimal rights and no possibility of gaining citizenship.

Immigrants with Physical and Mental Disabilities

Over the course of the nineteenth century and much of the twentieth century, the exclusion of immigrants and refugees based on physical or mental impairments was mandated by federal law and upheld by the judicial branch of the U.S. government. Immigration laws in 1882 and 1891 established the stated policy of excluding potential immigrants with certain disabilities by barring entry of anyone who would be a public ward (Baynton, 2001). The immigration law passed in 1907 greatly expanded this method of exclusion by banning the immigration of any person with an impairment that might affect the ability to earn a living. These laws targeted people with mental, mobility, visual, and hearing impairments, and physical losses or deformities, as well as people who used assistive devices such as crutches or canes. By 1917, the list of physical conditions that could be used to exclude a potential immigrant included arthritis, asthma, blindness or poor eyesight, bunions, deafness, deformities of any sort, epilepsy, flat feet, heart disease, hernia, muteness, spinal curvature, varicose veins, and any other signs of slow or poor development (Baynton, 2001; Bulmer, 2003; Johnson, 2004). To assess if they had any of these conditions, potential immigrants arriving at Ellis Island were forced to climb steep staircases, perform tasks, and solve puzzles to demonstrate physical and sensory fitness, and were checked for signs of any potential disability. Hundreds of thousands of potential immigrants were identified as unfit by these tests and were turned away (Vinen, 2000).

The findings of mental and physical disabilities were rather aggressive, with one court holding that if there were any evidence whatsoever of mental or physical disability there should be "no hesitation" in refusing admission (*Ex parte Hosaye Sakaguchi*, 1922, p. 916). Courts also held that once an alien had been determined to be inadmissible for reasons of disability, the determination was conclusive and could not be rebutted by law (*United States ex. rel. Wulf v. Esperdy*, 1960). As a result, the doctrine of inadmissibility based on physical or mental disabilities—real, potential, or completely fabricated by immigration officials—was applied to a wide variety of aliens, many of whom did not even have documented or identifiable medical conditions. Some of the health problems that were cited as reasons for preventing immigration by some individuals seem rather strange, especially in cases that did not involve identifiable medical conditions. In one case, a woman was deemed inadmissible for being blind in one eye and having recurring sinus problems (*United States ex rel. Markin v. Curran*, 1925).

Starting in the late 1800s, many immigrants could even be excluded based on disabilities and conditions that were not initially identified by immigration officials (*Ex parte Wong Nung*, 1929; *Opinion of the Attorney General*, 1903). If a person with a disability was allowed to enter because immigration officials did not notice the disability, the admission could be revoked if the disability was later discovered (*United States v. Schwarz*, 1949). The courts gave immigration authorities tremendous latitude in making decisions of inadmissibility due to concerns about the physical health of the immigrant. This endorsement by the federal government for immigration officials to aggressively employ physical and mental health concerns to prevent immigration came at the height of one of the early waves of anti-immigration hysteria. Chapters of protectionist organizations like the Immigration Restriction League, "the 100 percenters," and the American Protective Association had begun to sprout around the nation, ultimately becoming popular groups with distressingly large followings (Boorstin, 1989; DeLaet, 2000). Members of the Immigration Restriction League, a group comprising intellectuals and community leaders, included the presidents of Harvard University, Stanford University, Georgia Institute of Technology, the University of Chicago, and the Wharton School of Finance, among others (Boorstin, 1989).

In the nineteenth and early twentieth centuries, the attitudes of the United States toward individuals with disabilities were still lagging compared to some other developed nations. For example, the United States was behind many European nations in providing educational opportunities to persons with disabilities. Denmark provided compulsory education for children with sensory impairments in 1817 (Hansen, 1916). By 1883, both France and England provided free primary education for children with disabilities (Winzer, 1993). In France, students with hearing impairments were first schooled in 1748, students with visual impairments in 1782, and students with mental impairments in 1832 (Winzer, 1993). In Canada, free compulsory education was first provided for children with hearing and visual impairments in the late 1880s (Winzer, 1993). The first American public schools offered segregated classes for students with disabilities in 1909, though nine states still did not permit education for blind students as late as 1930 and children with severe disabilities were still considered beyond education (Winzer, 1993). In 1948, only 12 percent of children with disabilities in the United States were receiving formal education (Ballard, Ramirez, & Weintraub, 1982). By 1962, only sixteen states educated children with mild mental impairments, and into the mid-1970s many states simply did not allow children with disabilities to attend public schools (Smith, 2001).

In the context of such a climate of discrimination, the efforts to exclude those with physical and mental disabilities from entering the country seem to match the general attitudes of the times. Someone who was deaf, mute, or both had little chance of being deemed admissible, as courts allowed immigration officials to assume that individuals with such impairments would become public wards if allowed to become citizens (*Tullman v. Tod*, 1923). Only by providing a great deal of evidence that he or she would not be a public charge could an individual with these types of impairments be considered admissible.

One man with a hearing impairment was able to immigrate after demonstrating that he was able to support himself as an experienced tailor, that he had a brother and an uncle who were both very successful business owners with a great deal of money, and that both the uncle and the brother were willing to look after him if the need arose (*United States v. Tod*, 1923). The reasons for this extensive demonstration of support, beyond pure discrimination, are hard to discern. The tailor had a business valued at $8,000 that produced $100 a week in income, owned a $20,000 equity interest in a property worth three times that amount that produced $10,000 a year in income, and had $5,665 in savings (*United States v. Tod*, 1923). These values indicate that the tailor was financially very well off for the time. In spite of how well the tailor had demonstrated he could do financially, clearly showing he was not in danger of becoming a public charge, he was considered admissible only after his uncle testified, "we are to take care of him" and his brother testified, "my brother I will keep at my house" (pp. 822–824). Even though his financial status indicated that he was better prepared to care for himself than most people trying to immigrate, he was nearly prevented from entering the country based solely on his hearing loss.

The history of preventing immigration based on perceived mental disabilities is perhaps the most striking. The Office of the Attorney General of the United States created mental health standards for immigration stating that any person found to be a "lunatic" and "idiot" or mentally "unable to take care of himself or herself without becoming a public charge" could never be allowed in the country (*Opinion of the Attorney General*, 1886). Later statements by the Office of the Attorney General affirmed these far-reaching and ill-defined standards (*Opinion of the Attorney General*, 1891a, b). As a result, immigration officials, with the full support of the courts, classified everything from mental retardation to homosexuality to abnormal behavior to the tendency to have seizures to simple low intellect as a mental disability that would prevent immigration. As with the physical disability classification, mental disability classifications were used, under the disguise of concern for public health or concern for admitting public charges, as a tool to discriminate against individuals with disabilities who wished to become U.S. citizens.

Based on immigration laws, courts held that any individual with a "psychopathic" or "inferior mental state," or an "idiot" or someone likely to become a "public charge" due to his or her mental state had to be excluded from immigrating to the United States (*United States v. Schwarz*, 1949). This broad category included those suffering from a "mental defect," those with a "psychopathic personality," and even those with epilepsy (*Boutilier v. Immigration and Naturalization Service*, 1966). Many of these diagnoses of mental impairment were made with IQ tests, which were intentionally designed to be culturally and linguistically biased to ensure that most immigrants, except those from western Europe, would be judged inferior and therefore undesirable (Branson & Miller, 2002; Gould, 1996). It was also established that public officials, including executive officers of the federal government, had no ability to alter findings by immigration officials that aliens were mentally inferior and therefore inadmissible to the United States (*United States ex rel. Patton v. Tod*, 1924). The court summarized this policy by writing, "the executive officers of the government have no discretion whatsoever to admit to the United States a person duly found to be an imbecile" (*United States ex rel. Patton v. Tod*, 1924, p. 395).

If an alien was found to be suffering from a mental disability at the time of entry into the United States, it was presumed that the alien, if allowed to immigrate, would, without exception, become a public charge (*Gegiow v. Uhl*, 1915; *United States ex rel. Mandel v. Day*, 1927). The courts endorsed the belief that a person with "mental abnormalities," which were thought to lead to "moral deficiencies," could only fall into poverty and become the responsibility of the state (*Ex parte Fragoso*, 1926, p. 989). Though these terms are incredibly unspecific and malleable, the courts continued to support their use well into the second half of the twentieth century as valid (*Boutilier v. Immigration and Naturalization Service*, 1966).

Courts have the power to invalidate a statute that is unconstitutionally vague. A law is void if it is so vague that people "of common intelligence must necessarily guess at its meaning and differ as to its application" (*Connolly v. General Construction Co.*, 1926, p. 391). However, courts took no action under the vagueness doctrine regarding these cases, despite the fact that the standards related to physical and mental disabilities were ill-defined and allowed immigration officials to make decisions with no supervision or review. The drive to prevent immigration by persons with disabilities even led to legal restrictions on the number of immigrants from specific countries of origin. The immigration law passed in 1924 was designed to specifically limit the immigration of persons from countries that were more likely to produce people with mental disabilities, as indicated by studies of IQ scores among immigrants (Gould, 1996).

Even those trying to immigrate with someone who was deemed to have a mental disability might not be allowed to enter the United States. A woman was found to be suffering from "mongolism" (the common and highly racist term used at the time for people with Down syndrome) and deemed inadmissible, as was her perfectly healthy mother, who had the ill fortune of trying to immigrate with her own daughter (*United States ex rel. Saclarides v. Shaughnessy*, 1950). Presumably the mother would not have wanted to enter the country if her daughter could not, but it is striking that the mother was found inadmissible simply because her daughter had a mental disability.

Someone who had previously had a disabling condition, but who had recovered by the time of attempted immigration, could also be excluded from entering the country (*In re Hollinger*, 1962). A "previous attack of insanity," no matter how far distant in the past, was deemed sufficient to bar entry to the United States (p. 205). An alien deemed to have mental health problems during one attempt to enter the United States, but not experiencing any mental health problems at the time of a second, much later, attempt to enter the country, could also be excluded from entering the United States (*In re Hollinger*, 1962). The exclusion of persons with mental disabilities is particularly harsh given that the process of immigration can be so stressful that it has a temporary impact on mental health (Berger, 2001; Portes & Rumbaut, 1996).

In short, someone could be excluded from the United States if thought to have any kind of physical or sensory impairment, physical abnormality or deformity, developmental limitation, or hereditary or contagious condition, or if thought to be a lunatic, an epileptic, an idiot, unable to provide personal care, stupid, insane, previously insane, simply not very bright, or having the potential to be in any of these states. These tremendously open-ended standards were used to prevent untold numbers of potential immigrants with disabilities from gaining admission to the United States. The vagueness of these standards was also perfect for use as a tool of discrimination both against persons with disabilities and against other groups.

Disability as an Excuse to Exclude Aliens
from Specific Countries

The laws and policies meant to exclude persons with disabilities were often used as a way to exclude other groups who were deemed socially undesirable. At times, these policies were used to keep out disproportionate numbers of immigrants from African nations, Greece, Hungary, Italy, Japan, Poland, Portugal, Russia, Syria, and other nations, as well as Jewish immigrants, by asserting that these groups of people were more likely to be physically or mentally disabled (Baynton, 2001; Gould, 1996; Pfeiffer, 1999; Portes & Rumbaut, 1996). In such cases, the ideas of eugenics that only certain people should be allowed to reproduce were interpreted to mean that only certain people should even be allowed into society. Supporters of eugenics were, not surprisingly, strong supporters of restrictions on immigration (Gillham, 2001; Richards, 1987; Ridley, 1999).

Of all the groups considered undesirable as immigrants in the nineteenth and early twentieth centuries, individuals from Asia in general, and from China in particular, seem to have faced some of the most difficult circumstances with immigration officials inclined to use concerns about disability as a reason to prevent entry to the United States (Chen, 1990; Fetzer, 2000; Kitano & Daniels, 2001; Park, 2004). Anti-Chinese sentiment was considerable, with lynching, murders, and race riots being common occurrences (Kitano & Daniels, 2001). Although at no time in the nineteenth century did the population of immigrants from China in the United States exceed 125,000, fears about the potential number of Chinese immigrants and their economic power led to the restriction of most immigration from China (Kitano & Daniels, 2001). An 1882 law drastically limiting entry and settlement of Chinese citizens in the United States legalized anti-Chinese discrimination (Fetzer, 2000; Park, 2004). The law suspended most immigration from China for a ten-year period and had "an elaborate system of registration, certification, and identification with imprisonment and deportation as penalties for violation and fraud" (Tsai, 1983, pp. 65–68). This policy virtually excluded anyone from China, except for visiting merchants and their families, from even entering the country, and the courts upheld these laws (*Lau Ow Bew v. U.S.*, 1892; *United States v. Gue Lim*, 1899).

Those Chinese who could still legally enter the United States under the exclusion laws often discovered that physical or mental disabilities were a convenient way for the U.S. government to extend exclusion beyond the scope of the laws. Numerous court decisions about various reasons for denying admission from the mid-nineteenth to the early twentieth century focused specifically on the fact that the aliens at issue were from China (*Ex parte Lee Sher Wing*, 1908; *Ex parte Li Dick*, 1909; *Looe Shee v. North*, 1909). Some of these cases actually involved unspecific references to disabilities, but did include particular emphasis on the nation of origin of the aliens (*Ex parte Li Dick*, 1909).

Some cases involving Chinese aliens go so far as to quote the statute stating those with disabilities are inadmissible, and use this as a reason for barring entry of the alien, without even stating the nature of the disability of the alien at issue (*Ex parte Li Dick*, 1909). The suspicious emphasis on excluding Chinese immigrants for disabilities was further reinforced by an opinion from the Office of the Attorney General that openly encouraged the exclusion of Asian aliens for undocumented, potential disabilities (*Opinion of the Attorney General*, 1903). Chinese aliens were even considered inadmissible if they had a contagious disease that they caught after landing in the United States (*Ex parte Wong Nung*, 1929). In cases with a documented physical ailment of a Chinese alien, the reasons for refusing admission could be incredibly weak. A young man from China was denied admission for having trachoma (*Ex parte Lee Sher Wing*, 1908). Trachoma is a type of conjunctivitis that results in inflammation of the eyelids; though contagious, it is hardly a major health problem. A court's opinion in another case from the same time period actually described trachoma as "a very common disease with children... readily curable in a few days or weeks" (*In re Di Simone*, 1901, p. 946). It is hard to see how trachoma could pose an overwhelming threat to public health, but this individual was barred from entering the United States for having crusty eyelids.

Homosexuality as Mental Disability

While physical disabilities seemed to be the method of choice by government officials to exclude immigrants from China, mental disabilities have been used as the method of choice to exclude another group of potential immigrants. In the case of mental disabilities, the clearest targets of discrimination have been the members of the gay community. Immigration laws prevented people with "psychopathic personalities" from entering the United States. Historically, the term "psychopathic personalities" was interpreted to include individuals who evidenced homosexual tendencies (Morris, 1980). Under this policy, psychiatrists of the U.S. Public Health Service were required to officially certify aliens evidencing homosexual tendencies as psychopathic. These suspect aliens were subjected to full psychological examinations to determine whether they were to be certified as homosexual, foreclosing the possibility of their immigration to the United States (Morris, 1980). The Supreme Court fully endorsed this policy, ruling that deporting aliens with homosexual tendencies was not a constitutional violation (*Rosenberg v. Fleutti*, 1963; *Boutilier v. Immigration and Naturalization Services*, 1966). Immigration officers were even trained to watch for a litany of suspected homosexual traits in aliens; under these standards, seeming too educated, cultured, or well-groomed left men open to being suspected of having homosexual tendencies (Morris, 1980).

The policy of excluding aliens with homosexual tendencies as having a mental disability solely based on their sexual preference actually continued into the 1980s before being stopped by court orders (*Lesbian/Gay Freedom Day Committee, Inc. v. U.S. I.N.S.*, 1982). In that case, the court finally held that homosexuality alone, in the absence of any "medically recognized and certified mental disorder" or any "sexual deviation," did not meet the reasonableness standard because medical professionals did not recognize homosexuality by itself to be a mental disorder or a sexual deviation (*Lesbian/ Gay Freedom Day Committee, Inc. v. U.S. I.N.S.*, 1982). By linking their homophobia to the threat of disability, the people seeking to exclude homosexuals from immigrating to the United States were employing a trick of using disability to make a group of people seem more socially unacceptable, and thus easier to exclude.

IMMIGRATION POLICIES AS A REFLECTION OF SOCIAL ATTITUDES TOWARD DISABILITY

As examined in the preceding chapter, the United States has had a prolonged, tortured struggle to undo the shackles of discrimination against individuals with disabilities. Immigration laws and policies, over time, have been used as an excuse for keeping out certain socially unpopular groups, such as individuals with disabilities. In many ways, the evolution of immigration policies represents an interesting microcosm of the social phenomenon of disability discrimination. As in many other aspects of society, physical and mental disabilities have been the wellspring for social exclusion. For many, many years, people with physical and mental disabilities were simply excluded from immigrating to the country under most circumstances. Also, like many other areas in which discrimination against persons with disabilities has been a problem, these issues have not yet been resolved.

The laws and cases regarding inadmissibility decisions related to disability reflect a long-standing determination by lawmakers and immigration officials to exclude individuals with physical and mental disabilities. Aliens with physical or mental disabilities of all kinds were discriminated against in the admission process, with the discrimination being justified as protecting public health and preventing the creation of public charges. The United States, it must be noted, is far from alone in using immigration policies as a method to exclude persons with disabilities (Davis, 1999). However, discrimination against individuals with disabilities in U.S. immigration policies has one other aspect. Immigration policies have used the purported or feared presence of disability to exclude members of other groups who were socially unpopular at the time by claiming they might be more likely to have a disability. The subtext of such policies reveals that disability has been regarded, at least in terms of being allowed to enter a society, as basically the lowest level of human existence. Prior to changes in social attitudes that occurred in the late twentieth century, the classification of having a disability was equated with being unwelcome and unwanted.

A person who was considered socially unacceptable because he or she belonged to a particular group was something more than unacceptable if the person also had or might have a disability. An immigrant from China might have been unwelcome, but an immigrant from China who might have a disability could be excluded without a second thought. Immigrants with homosexual tendencies were unwanted, so the most efficient way to keep them out was to label homosexuality a mental disability. The addition of the claim of present or potential disability, whether founded or not, has historically often been enough to exclude immigrants, regardless of whatever other characteristics they may possess. In the case of people who were members of unpopular groups, the added claim of disability was a sufficient reason for exclusion that had basically no checks or balances.

The passage of disability rights laws, particularly the ADA, has curbed much of the discrimination against persons with disabilities in the immigration process (Johnson, 2004; Lyons, 1999; Stanton, 1996). However, persons with disabilities can still be barred from immigrating on the basis of being likely to become a public charge or if thought to present a risk of injury to others (Blakeman, 2000; Johnson, 2004). Also, immigrants with disabilities can not qualify for certain public benefits (Demleitner, 1997; Johnson, 2004). The classification of disability directly affected entry to the United States for untold tens and hundreds of thousands of individuals who sought access to the opportunities available in America. Other legal classifications of disability have an impact on many other forms of access. The complex interrelationships between access and legal classifications of disability are explored in part II.

II

Access and Accessibility

5

Physical Access, Intellectual Access, and Access in Society

Access is a multifaceted concept with impacts on every part of daily life. For individuals with disabilities, access can best be understood as the right to participate equally in ways that are not constrained by physical or mental limitations. Access can include entering and maneuvering around buildings, being allowed to actively and meaningfully participate in employment and other social functions, and employing assistive technology to use objects in a manner similar to people without disabilities. Many battles for access have focused on buildings, transportation, communication, and public environments (Barnartt & Scotch, 2001).

The social classifications of disability have significant relations to the access of individuals with disabilities to society as a whole and to the various activities that comprise a society. As chapter 4 demonstrated, for a person wishing to immigrate to the United States, being classified as having a disability historically prevented access, in the most holistic sense, to the United States. If persons with disabilities are socially excluded and classified as having little value, then few efforts are made by the society to provide equal access. When persons with disabilities are socially included and classified as having value, then issues of equal access become social concerns. Access to society for individuals with disabilities can be viewed in terms of physical access (e.g., to objects and places) and intellectual access (e.g., to ideas and information). These two forms of access are often interrelated, but each has unique characteristics.

Access as a mode of equality is a concept that often does not receive adequate consideration. A key reason is that society "still generally perceives all disability as a purely internal state" (Goering, 2002, p. 375), so the effect of social structures on individuals with disabilities is frequently ignored. The history of the accommodation of disabilities is almost exclusively related to physical objects and structures (Rebell, 1986). This focus on physical access may be explained by the fact that physical changes are easier to observe. If a store has a ramp to the door, people may feel that all the problems for patrons with disabilities have been addressed, regardless of whether patrons with disabilities are treated fairly by the staff or have equal access to what is inside the store.

Most of the legal cases related to disability rights have addressed issues of physical access in the broadest sense, such as the right to attend school (*Mills v. Board of Education*, 1972; *Pennsylvania Association for Retarded Children (PARC) v. Commonwealth of Pennsylvania*, 1971), serve on juries (*Galloway v. Superior Court of District of Columbia*, 1993), serve in the military (*Lane v. Pena*, 1996), be admitted to a professional organization (*Petition of Rubenstein*, 1994), take professional licensing exams (*Bartlett v. New York State Board of Law Examiners*, 1997; *D'Amico v. New York State Board of Bar Examiners*, 1993), and attend graduate school (*Pushkin v. Regents of the University of Colorado*, 1981). Physical access for persons with disabilities means an ability to be present, to be included, and to have the same opportunities as others through accommodation, through assistive technology, and, most important, through the elimination of discriminatory practices.

The best-known battle for access for persons with disabilities is probably in the arena of public education. A key principle from this struggle, and subsequent laws such as Individuals with Disabilities Education Act (IDEA), is that students with disabilities have the right to access public education. This right to access includes the right to physically access the school building, the right to access the materials used in the classroom, and the right to access extracurricular activities. This access also applies to the most inclusive environment possible. Under the requirements of IDEA, a student with a disability must be placed in the least restrictive environment (LRE) possible that still meets the educational needs of the student. The presumption of LRE is for educational access and inclusion, where a student with a disability is to be removed from the general educational environment only when "the nature or severity of the disability is such that education in regular classes with the use of supplementary aids and services cannot be satisfactorily achieved" (34 C.F.R. § 300.550(b)(2)).

In spite of such laws, equal access to public education is an ongoing struggle for persons with disabilities. Genuine equal access to education has been obstructed by policies that emphasize symbolism over actual compliance, by inadequate funding, by an emphasis on standards, and by disagreements over best practices (Ware, 2002). Further, considerations of equal access to public schools often neglect the needs of educators with disabilities, who often have great difficulty finding teaching positions or who are unable to find work at all, regardless of their qualifications and abilities (Breckenridge & Vogler, 2001; Jaeger & Bowman, 2002).

PHYSICAL ACCESS

Many of the rights that individuals with disabilities have fought for are rights to be allowed equal access to physical places, such as schools, workplaces, libraries, government offices, and commercial establishments. Further, accommodations for people with disabilities tend to be understood by other members of society in purely physical terms (Hahn, 1997). Oftentimes the accommodations that are provided do not necessarily work together, or at all, leaving a person with a disability to face "multiple systems that failed to interface with one another" (Ware, 2002, p. 147). Nevertheless, considerations of disability tend to focus primarily on physical access.

> I was going to a luncheon in a university's convocation center, a very public and highly frequented building on campus. It was a celebration of faculty, a holiday gathering, and little did I expect to encounter any physical barriers. I parked in the accessible parking space, entered the building through the electronic doors, and then searched the ground floor to find an elevator. When I finally asked a banquet supervisor, she took me to the linen room and up a service elevator into the kitchen, exiting into the canned tomatoes and fresh produce section. As we walked through the rows of dishes and food in various stages of preparation, I wondered what the president of the university would do if he found himself in this situation. How are you supposed to feel celebrated when you emerge from the kitchen into a festive ballroom?

As physically inaccessible public architecture has long served to reinforce the peripheral social classification of individuals with disabilities (Imrie, 1996), issues of physical access begin with whether a person with a disability can enter a physical space. Physical access can apply to buildings, rooms, open spaces, venues, stores, arenas, sports complexes, and myriad other physical spaces. Physical access includes more than just the ability to enter a physical space, however, as it also encompasses the ability to physically maneuver and reach things within spaces. To ensure "full equality of opportunity," equal physical access often requires "alterations to the environment that will make opportunities truly equal" (Goering, 2002, p. 375). Physical access to the front door of a multistory building that lacks elevators would be meaningless to persons with certain disabilities who still could not access the specific places where they need to go inside the building.

Imagine that you are a wheelchair user. You decide to go to the local grocery store and are pleasantly surprised to find a ramp, automatic doors, and easy entrance into the store. But once you get in the store, imagine your disappointment as you discover that the shelves are placed at a height that makes it impossible for you to reach many of the items. In such a case, you have physical access to the space (the grocery store) but you do not have physical access to the materials in the space (the specific groceries you would like to purchase). Such situations are far from uncommon, as the architectural structure of places reinforces the marginalization of disability. Typically, social spaces are "used to disable rather than enable" persons with disabilities (Gleeson, 1999, p. 1).

> A huge public building—the front entrance opens to a lobby with 12 steps going up and 12 steps going down—no elevator in sight. My wheelchair was not going anywhere and neither was I. Actually, I should have entered the side entrance, where I would have been greeted with a downward slope, two scts of wooden doors, a stairwell, a sharp corner, and then a hall on the lower level where I would find the building's only elevator, which worked occasionally.

Accessible routes into and within buildings often separate persons with disabilities from others in the structure or even completely hide persons with disabilities from view of other people (Siebers, 2003). Accessibility to physical structures is usually conceived in absolute terms—that is, whether accessibility exists, not whether it is done logically, practically, or optimally (Church & Marston, 2003). As a result, accessible routes often do not take the route that is most efficient, direct, or attuned to the actual needs of persons with disabilities. This absolutist approach to physical accessibility frequently leads to situations where the accessible route is unnecessarily longer, goes through more obstacles, and is simply harder to traverse for persons with various disabilities (Church & Marston, 2003).

> Designers and architects can be surprisingly inconsiderate when designing accessible parking spaces and ramps. Lila, a wheelchair user, was bewildered to find that the ramp onto the curb at her dentist's office was located almost 100 yards away from the parking spaces for persons with disabilities. She was even more bewildered when she went up the ramp and found that she had to go all the way back to get to the entrance. She was parked directly in front of the door, but had to travel five minutes to get into the office. Once inside, she asked the dentist about this bizarre design, and the dentist replied that she should be grateful that there was a ramp at all.

Given the ever-increasing importance of information in modern society, it is essential to consider access for persons with disabilities in terms of information. In the information age, lack of access to information has far-reaching consequences. Physical access can be viewed as access to any type of physical or electronic documents embodying information (Svenonius, 2000). For individuals with disabilities seeking information, physical access entails a much broader range of issues than it does for others, as access to documents may include issues of building design where physical documents are housed, document format (large print, Braille, audio, closed caption), and assistive technology for interacting with electronic documents. However, aside from a few writings (Cirillo & Danford, 1996; Jaeger, 2002; Mates, 1991; McNulty, 1999; Wright & Davie, 1991), insufficient consideration has been given to information access for persons with disabilities.

The literature that does exist about providing access for individuals with disabilities is almost entirely focused on issues of physical access. Yet these discussions miss the range of issues of intellectual access. Issues of physical access are usually straightforward and easy to understand, especially since they are often observable when one is paying attention. For the wheelchair user, add a ramp to the entrance of the building. For the visually impaired individual, offer information via large-print materials or on cassette. For hearing-impaired individuals, provide closed captioning and make sure someone on staff is fluent in sign language. Issues of intellectual access, as they are much harder to observe than issues of physical access, are more difficult to define, identify, and address in society.

INTELLECTUAL ACCESS

Intellectual access, most generally, is "access to information" contained in physical documents, electronic documents, or other conduits for information (Svenonius, 2000, p. 122). Intellectual access to information includes how the information is categorized, organized, displayed, and represented. Studying intellectual access can reveal the best ways to make information accessible by bringing the information seeker and the information together in the most efficient manner possible through representation of the available information sources. Intellectual access implies having sufficient information for critical thinking and exposure to diverse viewpoints (Pitts & Stripling, 1990). Intellectual access has been discussed in terms of many areas of information technology including websites, images, classification, catalogs and archives, government materials, periodicals, software, digital documents, and library services (Aschmann, 2002; Bednarek, 1993; Cary & Ogburn, 2000; Chen & Rasmussen, 1999; Comaromi, 1990; Dilevko & Dali, 2003; Gilliland, 1988; Intner, 1991; Mandel & Wolven, 1996; Rankin, 1992). None of these discussions of intellectual access, however, adequately addresses persons with disabilities.

Two studies (Deines-Jones, 1996; Neville & Datray, 1993) attempt to discuss intellectual access to information for persons with disabilities. Neither makes an attempt to discuss anything beyond very practical issues, so they contribute little to a conceptual understanding of intellectual access for persons with disabilities. One study does mention the lack of research into intellectual access and individuals with disabilities (Deines-Jones, 1996). They do offer concrete examples of the importance of intellectual access to information for individuals with disabilities, with one study noting the need for assistive technologies being available and the importance of "equal intellectual access" (Neville & Datray, 1993, p. 71).

Intellectual access to information for persons with disabilities, at a more conceptual level, entails equal opportunity to understand intellectual content and pathways to that content. Neuroscientists have found that the brains of people with sensory or mobility disabilities may function in unique ways when learning and communicating, particularly when employing sign language or Braille to access information (Pinker, 2002). These unique ways of functioning certainly may have an impact on intellectual access for persons with sensory and mobility disabilities. For individuals with learning disabilities, intellectual access is a keenly important issue, as their ability to understand certain content may hinge on how it is organized and represented. For example, if information on a Web site is poorly organized and cluttered, the content of the site will be intellectually inaccessible to people with certain learning disabilities. Clarity in organization and representation is similarly essential for intellectual access for individuals with cognitive disabilities. Intellectual access is also important for persons with physical disabilities. If organization or representation of information relies on visual cues, persons with visual impairments will not likely be able to intellectually access the information.

This concept is shaped by the fact that individuals with disabilities, as a group, approach information differently than other people, as a result of differences in cognition, communication, and social conditioning. From a cognitive standpoint, research indicates that individuals with disabilities, due to the need to make continual adaptations in their daily lives, often understand and approach activities and information in different ways than individuals who do not have disabilities (Gill, 1995; Samure & Given, 2004). Individuals with disabilities also tend to approach communication with a different focus than other individuals (Gill, 1995). These differences in cognition and communication have obvious relevance to intellectual access, as nontraditional modes of cognition and communication mean that the ways in which persons with disabilities organize, understand, and retrieve information may often differ from the ways that other individuals do the same things.

In regard to social conditioning, individuals with disabilities are classified in specific ways by societies (Davis, 1997, 2000; Frank, 1988; Gill, 2001; Rioux, 1994). These social classifications shape how individuals with disabilities view themselves and what they are personally capable of (Berube, 1997; Frank, 1988). The ways in which others treat individuals with disabilities is directly tied to social classifications as well (Berube, 1997; Frank, 1988). It seems conceivable that these social pressures will impact how individuals with disabilities organize, understand, and retrieve information. If this is the case, it represents a further uniqueness in how individuals with disabilities intellectually access information.

Another layer of differences in intellectual access relates to specific disabilities. Certain disabilities, most specifically learning disabilities, can greatly affect how the individual organizes and understands information and pathways to information. Courts have worked to ensure that the legal rights of individuals with disabilities are applied so that they include the needs of individuals with learning disabilities, especially in educational settings (*Guckenberger v. Boston University*, 1997).

Abby is a junior in high school with a learning disability that affects her ability to spell. She is not a bad speller, it just takes her longer to order the letters in her head and get them down on paper. She is smart and has always been a good student, so she is taking several advanced placement courses. Though her learning disability has been diagnosed and her teachers are aware of it, not all teachers seem to remember to take it into consideration by allowing her a little extra time to complete written tasks. Nevertheless, she is earning high grades in all but one of her classes.

This school year, Abby has had to gently remind her language arts teacher of her need for extra time on spelling tests. This particular teacher does not believe that learning disabilities really exist, so she is refusing to consider Abby's condition, which is naturally hurting Abby's performance in the class. Upon being reminded of Abby's learning disability after a fourth consecutive spelling test, the language arts teacher told Abby that she will have to realize sooner or later that she has trouble spelling because she is stupid. The teacher then told Abby that if she mentioned her learning disability one more time, the teacher would have Abby placed in a remedial class.

The combination of these unique factors for persons with disabilities demonstrates that a disability will affect how an individual intellectually accesses information. The relationship between intellectual access and individuals with disabilities has been relatively absent in academic discourse. However, it is of utmost importance for intellectual access to be an equal partner of physical access in efforts to provide equal access for individuals with disabilities. It does no good for a screen to be made readable if the user still cannot access the information on the screen. Similarly, any theoretical understanding of intellectual access, to be inclusive of the information needs of all, should account for the roles disability can play in intellectual access.

PHYSICAL ACCESS, INTELLECTUAL ACCESS, AND THE INFORMATION AGE

Social classifications help shape how individuals with disabilities conceive of access, affecting how they intellectually access entities. These social classifications also determine how physical and intellectual access is provided to individuals with disabilities by socially defining the rights of individuals with disabilities and influencing legal classifications of who has a disability.

However, in spite of public policies and laws that mandate equal access for persons with disabilities, people often do not understand the genuine importance of equal access. For example, educators in public schools, who must often work with students with disabilities, frequently have no comprehension of the reasons for equal access and inclusion for students with disabilities or the social benefits of such access (Ware, 2002).

With the growing importance of the Internet and other forms of information technology, equal access to electronic information and services has become an important new area of concern for social justice where the disadvantaged are often those "who have fought for civil rights in other areas of our society" (First & Hart, 2002, p. 385). For individuals with disabilities, the primary issue is the need for full accessibility. "Information is power, and a healthy democracy must guarantee access to this information and power equally for all of its citizens" (Hawthorne, Denge, & Coombs, 1997, n.p.). Equal access for individuals with disabilities is the "right thing to do. This out-weighs issues of cost, nationality, and adoption time" (Guenther, 2002, p. 72).

An item is accessible "if it can be used in a variety of ways that do not depend on a single sense or ability" (Nadler & Furman, 2001, p. 14). As a result, for an item to be fully accessible, it must be able to produce similar outcomes or results for any user, regardless of any impairment that the user might have. A screen-reading program, for example, verbalizes the content displayed on a computer screen so that a person with a visual impairment can hear the information that he or she is unable to see. Also, technologies "must be flexible enough to work with the various assistive technology devices that a person with a disability might use and to provide relevant content in an accessible modality" (Lazar, Beere, Greenridge, & Nagappa, 2003, p. 331). An estimated 13.1 million Americans use some kind of assistive technology, such as screen enlargement devices or voice synthesizers, on a daily basis (Johnson, 2004). A disability alters how an individual approaches and deals with any entity. Accessibility allows individuals with disabilities to have use of information and services that is equal or equivalent to the use enjoyed by everyone else. Accessibility to information and communication technologies (ICTs) encompasses issues of both physical and intellectual access.

Accommodations to create full physical accessibility are commonplace—the wheelchair ramp to the front door, the TDD (Telephonic Device for the Deaf) number, and the Braille menu. In terms of information, intellectual accessibility becomes a matter of ensuring that individuals with disabilities are not prevented from being able to access the information that everyone else is able to access. Individuals with disabilities, due to the factors noted above, are vulnerable to problems with intellectual access. These problems are reflected in the organization and understanding of information. Given the growing importance of information technology in the organization and retrieval of information, this area is a particular concern for individuals with disabilities. Even though "[i]t is imperative that all Americans have access to the technologies of tomorrow," individuals with disabilities have some of the lowest levels of computer and Internet usage in the entire American population (Kennard & Lyle, 2001, p. 5).

A large part of this discrepancy in access is due to the failure to consider accessibility for persons with disabilities in ICTs. Accessibility for people with disabilities has been frequently neglected in the development of ICTs (Goggin & Newell, 2000; Kanayama, 2003; Ransom, 1994). ICTs have usually been developed without regard to accessibility, leaving many individuals with disabilities excluded from use of the technologies unless appropriate assistive technologies are developed (Stephanidis & Savidis, 2001). Advances in ICTs have often created new "barriers for people with disabilities" (Department of Justice, 2001, p. 1). As a result, the level of computer usage and Internet access by individuals with disabilities is half that of the rest of the population (Department of Commerce, 2000). At this point, if the design process of an ICT attempts to account for considerations of users with disabilities, developers often employ the principles of usability, which focus on typical users, in place of considerations of accessibility (Keates & Clarkson, 2003). However, usability principles are inappropriate substitutes for accessibility principles (Keates & Clarkson, 2003).

Though some of this neglect is a result of lack of understanding of the needs of individuals with disabilities in the design process, policies have often been formulated with intent to exclude people with disabilities (Goggin & Newell, 2000; Keates & Clarkson, 2003). For example, policy discussions of universal access to technologies do not sufficiently account for disability (Stephanidis & Savidis, 2001). Further, potential extra costs have been frequently cited as a reason for not making inclusive technologies or policies (Bowe, 1993; Kanayama, 2003). This trend dates back to the development of the first telephone networks, when the needs of hearing-impaired individuals were disregarded due to perceived costs (Lang, 2000).

New technologies often present problems for persons with disabilities. Sometimes, this is not a problem because you can find alternate ways of accomplishing the same thing. There are times, unfortunately, when finding a viable alternative is not possible, particularly when a technology quickly becomes omnipresent in society. As technology is becoming more commonplace and inescapable in the information society, more inaccessible technological devices are becoming commonplace.

A prime example of this situation is the little boxes for credit cards and debit cards that now seem to be at almost every checkout lane in stores around the country. The boxes save the stores time by having the customer make the credit or debit transaction. However, the touch screens are small, use small type and have dark backgrounds, are placed on the counter, and require dexterity to use. For individuals with a number of different disabilities, these little boxes are very difficult to use. Consider:

- For persons with visual impairments, the screens are pretty much unreadable.
- For persons who use wheelchairs or who are small in stature, the boxes are unreachable.
- For persons with mental disabilities, the instructions given by the device may be hard to understand.
- For persons with learning disabilities, it may take a long time to read and process what is on the screen.
- For persons with mobility impairments, it may be hard or impossible to use the touch screen.

None of these problems, of course, occur when you are able to simply hand your credit card to the cashier.

Accessibility is important for a number of socially significant reasons. The capacities to transmit, access, and receive information are key components of citizenship (Sparks, 1993; Williams, 1963), and democratic governments have an interest in providing access to all citizens (Hammond, 2002; Kennard & Lyle, 2001). An inaccessible ICT turns a physical disability into a social disability (Goggin & Newell, 2000). A hearing impairment coupled with an inaccessible phone system, for example, results in virtual exclusion from telephony and all of the roles telephone communication can play in everyday life. Limited access to ICTs also increases the possibility that people with disabilities will have a harder time being able to get highly skilled positions, as for some people with disabilities, accessible ICTs are essential to their work (Dispenza, 2002; Schartz, Schartz, & Blanck, 2002).

Accessible technologies also frequently benefit people beyond those that the technologies were originally designed to help. Telephones, typewriters, scanners, closed-captioning, keyboard shortcuts for computer commands, modems, voice-activated software, synthesized text readers, and many other technologies were originally designed with the needs of various groups of individuals with disabilities in mind. When technologies cross over from being assistive technologies for persons with disabilities to widely used modern conveniences, even those people who do not support accommodations for persons with disabilities stop viewing such technologies as unnecessary or unduly expensive (Lacheen, 2000).

For many, accessible ICTs represent "an opportunity to join the workforce" for the first time (Rich et al., 2002, p. 51). Ninety percent of persons with disabilities who use accessible technologies at work report that they are able to do their jobs more efficiently and more effectively (Johnson, 2004). Such accessible ICTs may actually provide a way to help overcome the staggering social barriers to employment that many individuals with disabilities have faced historically (Jenkins, 1991; Scotch & Schriner, 1997; Yelin, 1992). Greater inclusion in the workforce may serve to foster increased inclusion in other areas of society (Oliver & Barnes, 1998). On the other hand, a lack of access to socially important ICTs, such as telephony or the Internet, can lead to the potential for social alienation (Jacko & Hanson, 2002; Jaeger, 2004b; Jaeger & Thompson, 2004).

More emphasis on accessible technologies also could make a tremendous difference to students with disabilities in higher education. Though IDEA and the Rehabilitation Act have provided a means by which accessible technologies have become a part of elementary and secondary schools, many colleges and universities lag far behind in providing accessible technologies for students with disabilities. As more colleges and universities use online course materials, offer distance education classes, and incorporate new technologies into coursework, accessibility becomes an increasingly significant issue to ensure equal access for persons with disabilities. However, many school Web sites are inaccessible and many schools lack any policies on accessibility, seriously inhibiting the ability of students with disabilities to be full participants in their own courses (Carlson, 2004; Wattenberg, 2004). Such inaccessibility even prevents some faculty members from fully participating in the online courses they teach (Abram, 2003).

For individuals with disabilities, equal access in general has always been a concern. Access must be both mandated by policy and actually available. "A vast gap remains between the rhetoric of public inclusion that mandates everything from universal design to inclusive classrooms and the battles that still have to be fought on a daily basis to ensure their availability—battles which not everyone can or will fight" (Rapp & Ginsburg, 2001, p. 541). Further, the actual levels of accessibility of ICTs for individuals with specific disabilities remain mostly untested, as most studies of accessibility focus on accessibility in general and do not examine accessibility of ICTs for individuals with different types of disabilities (Jaeger, 2003b). Without such data, it is not known if accessibility problems with particular ICTs are greatest for individuals with mobility impairments or visual impairments or other types of disability. Physical access and intellectual access, given the opportunities presented by new forms of electronic information and ICTs, are issues that must receive much more consideration so that individuals with disabilities are not excluded from the information age (Jaeger, 2004b). As chapter 6 discusses, legal classifications of disability have great significance in establishing rights to equal access and will likely be very important in extending access into the age of the World Wide Web.

6

Access and Classifications of Disability in Legal Discourse

The earliest known legal classifications of individuals with disabilities date back to ancient Hebraic law (Stiker, 1999). Societies that based their legal systems on the Old Testament of the Bible also had legal classifications of disability (Daniels, 1997). The Roman Code of Justinian created a unified code of civil law for the empire that had a tremendous impact on laws of most of Europe into the eighteenth century. This code and the companion digests of Roman case law detailed many legal rights that individuals with certain types of disability were not allowed to have (Watson, 1998). Beginning in medieval times, English courts began using ad hoc tests to establish whether someone had a mental disability for cases involving personal independence, the right to inherit or own property, and other issues (Neugebauer, 1996; Rushton, 1996). These oral tests involved asking questions involving numeracy, orientation, and everyday communication; failing the test resulted in being legally classified as a fool, an idiot, or a lunatic (Neugebauer, 1996; Rushton, 1996). By the fifteenth century in England, persons with disabilities were legally classified as disabled in terms of their inability to work (Branson & Miller, 2002).

In spite of the widespread embrace of eugenics in the United States, the first legal classifications of persons with disabilities to provide broad affirmative rights arose in the United States in the mid to late twentieth century. Following the lead of the United States, a number of other nations adopted laws or amended their constitutions in the 1990s to provide the first real legal rights for individuals with disabilities (Metts, 2000). These nations include Austria, Australia, Brazil, Denmark, Finland, Germany, Malawi, the

Philippines, Sweden, South Africa, Uganda, the United Kingdom, Vene-zuela, and Zimbabwe (Metts, 2000). However, the nations that have created affirmative legal classifications of disability remain a distinct minority. "The social exclusion approach ('out of sight, out of mind') is still very prevalent in the world" (Albrecht & Verbugge, 2000, p. 299).

In the United States, the classifications of disability have become an ele-ment of policy discourse at the national level (Baker, 2002; Drimmer, 1993). The disability rights laws in the United States are more concerned with classifying disability than classifying discrimination. Rather than placing the emphasis on defining a disability, many other nations have disability rights laws that prioritize defining discrimination in terms of the barriers to in-clusion that are socially created. In some ways, the emphasis on social bar-riers is more sensible than the approach taken by the United States, because "a barrier in the person's environment typically plays a causal role in pro-ducing disability discrimination" (National Council on Disability, 2003a, p. 25). The laws of the United States, however, emphasize creating classi-fications of who qualifies as having a disability.

Three major federal laws, Section 504 of the Rehabilitation Act, the In-dividuals with Disabilities Education Act, and the Americans with Dis-abilities Act, offer definitions of who has a disability. These definitions are not uniform, creating differences in approaches to the legal classification of disability. The general classifications of disability under Section 504 and the ADA are similar. The classifications of disability from these two acts have been used in other antidiscrimination acts related to individuals with dis-abilities, such as the Fair Housing Act of 1988 and the Air Carrier Access Act of 1986. As each classification "valorizes some point of view and silences another" (Bowker & Star, 1999, p. 5), there are some salient differences between the legal classifications of disability. The differences between the laws impact the ways in which the laws promote social inclusion and provide for equal access to elements of society.

Anyone who has a disability that impacts the ability to navigate, such as a mobility or sensory impairment, is intimately familiar with the fact that many stores seem particularly inclined to make life difficult. As stores work to arrange merchandise so that customers have to pass as many items as possible, many stores now do not let people move in anything approximating a straight line. The more mazelike a store becomes, the harder it is for anyone with mobility or sensory problems to get through, all the while making one paranoid about knocking over a display, falling over an oddly placed item, or injuring oneself on a counter.

When stores intentionally employ a layout that resembles a labyrinth, it makes shopping extremely difficult for many individuals with disabilities. In fact, a large number of persons with disabilities simply refuse to enter these types of stores because of how unsafe they are. The law may call for accessible buildings, but many stores seem to be striving to be inaccessible inside the building.

PRIMARY CLASSIFICATIONS UNDER THE LAW

Section 504 of the Rehabilitation Act

The first broad, affirmative legal classification of individuals with disabilities in the United States was articulated by Section 504 of the Rehabilitation Act of 1973, which applies to the federal government and entities receiving federal funds. Under the Rehabilitation Act, an individual is classified as having a disability if the individual "(i) has a physical or mental impairment which substantially limits one or more major life activities, (ii) has a record of such an impairment, or (iii) is regarded as having such an impairment" (34 C.F.R. § 104.3(j)). Under Section 504, a major life activity is a function "such as caring for one's self, performing manual tasks, walking, seeing, hearing, breathing, learning, and working" (34 C.F.R. § 104.3(j)(2)). The physical and mental impairments that constitute disabilities under Section 504 are:

> any psychological disorder or condition, cosmetic disfigurement, or anatomical loss affecting one or more of the following body systems: neurological; musculoskeletal; special sense organs, respiratory, including speech organs; cardiovascular; reproductive, digestive, genito-urinary, hemic and lymphatic; skin and endocrine; or any mental or psychological disorder, such as mental retardation, organic brain syndrome, emotional or mental illness, and specific learning disabilities. (34 C.F.R. § 104.3(j))

This list is not even exhaustive. One court held that Section 504 protects individuals with any condition that substantially "weakens, diminishes, restricts, or otherwise damages an individual's health or physical or mental activity" (*E. E. Black Limited v. Marshall*, 1980, p. 1098).

Section 504 specifies that individuals who have conditions of homosexuality, bisexuality, transvestism, transsexuality, pedophilia, voyeurism, exhibitionism, kleptomania, compulsive gambling, pyromania, gender identity issues, and sexual behavior disorders cannot be classified as having a disability. Further, Section 504 does not classify anyone who has "environmental, cultural, or economic disadvantages" unaccompanied by a physical or mental impairment as having a disability (34 C.F.R. § 104, appendix A). Individuals who are slow learners, of low intellectual caliber, or behind for their grade level but do not have a diagnosed mental impairment are also not classified as having a disability (United States Commission on Civil Rights, 1997). Negative personality traits such as poor judgment, irresponsible behavior, and poor self-control are not classified as disabilities under Section 504 (*Daley v. Koch*, 1986).

The Americans with Disabilities Act

The ADA prohibits discrimination against persons with disabilities by a wide range of private and public institutions, including many facets of local government, state government, and business. Similar to the Rehabilitation Act, the ADA classifies individuals as having a disability for: (1) having a physical or mental impairment that substantially limits one or more of the individual's major life activities, (2) having a record of such an impairment, or (3) being regarded as having such an impairment. Major life activities under the ADA include "caring for oneself, performing manual tasks, walking, seeing, hearing, speaking, breathing, learning and working," as well as sitting, standing, lifting, reaching, and engaging in mental or emotional processes such as "thinking, concentrating, and interacting with others" (29 C.F.R. § 1630.2(i)). An individual who is substantially limited in a major life activity is unable to perform that activity at all or can only perform the activity in severely limited fashion compared to other individuals performing the same activity. The ADA also mandates that the level of protection required by Section 504 is the minimum level of protection required by the ADA.

A physical or mental impairment, according to the Department of Justice regulations for enforcement of the ADA, is "any physiological disorder or condition, cosmetic disfigurement, or anatomical loss" affecting any one or more major body systems, such as sensory functioning or neurological functioning, and "[a]ny mental or psychological disorder" (28 C.F.R. § 35.104). Some of the conditions that have been commonly classified as disabilities under the ADA include hearing, visual, and mobility impairments, multiple sclerosis, muscular dystrophy, chronic fatigue, immune dysfunction syndrome, Crohn's disease, and cardiac problems (Jaeger & Bowman, 2002).

As with Section 504 of the Rehabilitation Act, lawmakers seem to have been keenly interested in deciding what is not classified as a disability. Under the ADA, a varied list of specific conditions cannot be classified as disabilities under any circumstances: homosexuality, bisexuality, transvestism, transsexualism, pedophilia, exhibitionism, voyeurism, gender identity disorders not resulting from physical impairments, any other sexual behavior disorders, pyromania, compulsive gambling, kleptomania, current alcoholism, obesity, and psychoactive substance use disorders resulting from the current illegal use of drugs.

Individuals with Disabilities Education Act

IDEA, as it deals specifically with the educational rights of students with disabilities, is devoted to classifying conditions that may impact educational processes. Annually, approximately 10 percent of students attending public school are protected by IDEA (Hallenbeck & Kauffman, 1994). Usually, more than 5 million children with disabilities are receiving some form of special education at any time (Vanderwood, McGrew, & Ysseldyke, 1998). The law classifies an extensive list of conditions as disabilities:

> mental retardation, hearing impairments including deafness, speech or language impairments, visual impairments including blindness, serious emotional disturbance,

orthopedic impairments, autism, traumatic brain injury, other health impairments, or specific learning disabilities. (20 U.S.C.A. § 1401(3)(A))

By including a specific list of what conditions are classified as disabilities under IDEA, there is a reduction of doubt as to who is protected by the statute. However, some groups have felt certain conditions were inappropriately excluded from the list. For example, there has been some controversy as to whether attention deficit disorder (ADD) or attention-deficit/hyperactivity disorder (ADHD) should be added to this list. Legislation to have ADD or ADHD added to the list has not succeeded, and the Department of Education has found no reason to place ADD or ADHD on the list since they could be classified under "other health impairments" (Jaeger & Bowman, 2002). A unique element of the classification of students with disabilities under IDEA is that the law is designed to provide special education and related services based on the individual needs of each student. Under IDEA, an individualized educational program has to be created to meet the specific needs of each student with a disability and reviewed annually.

LAWS AFFECTING ACCESS

Equal physical and intellectual access is essential for individuals with disabilities to have equal rights. The U.S. federal government has passed a number of disability rights laws related to access to a wide range of elements of society, including education, employment, physical structures, technologies, and commercial establishments. The U.S. government has, in fact, evidenced a "continual commitment to citizens with disabilities and their right to the same level of access" as all other citizens (Muir & Oppenheim, 2002b, p. 270). The laws demonstrate progress toward ensuring some form of access to the most important functions of society. A number of the disability rights laws even have application in cyberspace. Australia is the only other government to make concerted attempts to promote online accessibility thus far (Muir & Oppenheim, 2002b). The combined weight of all of these laws makes a powerful argument for a federal mandate of equal access for individuals with disabilities (Jaeger, 2004a). There are many other laws related to disability beyond those discussed herein (see Turnbull, Wilcox, Stowe, & Umbrager, 2001), but the ones detailed below are the primary laws that dictate the classifications of disability and the scope of access accorded by those classifications. Overall, the passage of these laws demonstrates a growing social acknowledgement of the civil rights of persons with disabilities (Drimmer, 1993).

The Architectural Barriers Act

The Architectural Barriers Act of 1968 was the first federal law mandating some form of equal access for individuals with disabilities. This law was focused exclusively on the design of structures, prioritizing physical accessibility in the construction of new buildings and modification or reconstruction of buildings built after 1968. The law mandates that buildings be built or altered to allow individuals with physical disabilities to be able to have equal access to all areas and services of the structure. It was the first step in creating a mandate of equal access for individuals with disabilities. Part of the Architectural Barriers Act was the creation of the Access Board, which is still responsible for creating recommended accessibility guidelines for the federal government (Peterson, 1998). The Access Board establishes design criteria for accessibility and develops and maintains accessibility requirements for physical environment, transportation, telecommunications equipment, and information technology for federal agencies.

Section 504 of the Rehabilitation Act

Section 504 of the Rehabilitation Act of 1973, which covers the federal government and entities receiving federal funds, first established the general standards of equal access for individuals with disabilities. Section 504 directs, "No otherwise qualified individual with a disability in the United States . . . shall, solely by reason of her or his disability, be excluded from the participation in, be denied the benefits of, or be subjected to discrimination under any program or activity receiving Federal financial assistance" (29 U.S.C.A. § 794). The basic requirements of the Rehabilitation Act mandate accessibility to the information, services, and locations of the federal government and to organizations receiving federal funds, such as public schools and state government agencies. The requirements of Section 504 also establish the first implication of a right to accessible information and communication technologies (Kanayama, 2003). Section 504 extends to equal participation in all federal government programs, which now includes government presence on the World Wide Web. The equal participation requirements of Section 504 also apply to the recipients of many types of federal funds, meaning that a local or state government receiving these types of funds may also be bound to the concept of equal participation for individuals with disabilities. These requirements provide the primary foundation for the rights established for persons with disabilities.

Individuals with Disabilities Education Act

IDEA, originally titled the Education for all Handicapped Children Act of 1974, ensures equal access to public education for all school-age individuals with disabilities. IDEA guarantees a free appropriate public education to students with disabilities up to their graduation from high school (Fleischer & Zames, 2001; Huefner, 1998; Jaeger & Bowman, 2002; Smith, 2001). IDEA guarantees that all students with disabilities have the legal right to receive an education in a public school that meets the individual needs of the student in as inclusive a setting as possible. Part of this set of protections is equal access to the benefits of public schooling. School materials and facilities, including textbooks, computers, and buildings, must be accessible to students with disabilities.

The act prioritizes access to the most typical educational situation possible by integrating students with disabilities into general education classrooms to the maximum extent feasible. IDEA compels schools to place students with disabilities in the least restrictive environment possible and to integrate students with disabilities into classes along with students without disabilities as frequently as possible. IDEA also includes due process requirements and appeal procedures to protect the rights of equal access or students with disabilities. Under IDEA, each student with a disability is guaranteed access to a free appropriate public education. This concept encompasses the special education, related services, and the requirements of the individualized education plan of the student with a disability.

For students with disabilities, the psychological benefits of equal access are enormous. The historical practice of denying children with disabilities equal access to education resulted in students with disabilities being undereducated, socially stigmatized, and emotionally traumatized (Arnold & Dodge, 1994; Hill, 1986; Stick, 1976). IDEA has certainly increased access to general education classrooms for students with disabilities. Since 1990, the number of students with disabilities educated in general education classrooms has increased consistently, while the number of students with disabilities in resource rooms has declined (McLesky, Henry, & Hodges, 1998). All students with disabilities have not shared in this progress, as students with mild disabilities are still more likely to be educated in general education classrooms than students with more profound disabilities (Hobbs & Westling, 1998). Overall, though, the accessibility provisions of IDEA extended the mandate of equal access into education, contributing to and reinforcing the focus of federal disability law on access.

Americans with Disabilities Act

The ADA prohibits discrimination against persons with disabilities by various private and public institutions. The ADA was designed to mandate equal access for individuals with disabilities in situations not covered by Section 504 of the Rehabilitation Act, such as state governments, local governments, and private businesses. Until the passage of the ADA in 1990, Congress failed to comprehensively address issues of equal access in society for persons with disabilities on a general level. The areas of access covered by the ADA include businesses, stores, housing, lodging, places of entertainment and public gathering, higher education, recreation facilities, social service centers, and transportation facilities. The areas of employment, public accommodations, and state and local government functions are the most obvious and frequent places of access that the ADA addresses. The ADA has provided very broad means of promoting access for persons with disabilities to a wide range of elements of society.

Television Decoder Circuitry Act

Enacted in 1990, the Television Decoder Circuitry Act established the requirement that television set manufacturers install the appropriate technology to allow televisions to display closed-captioning signals. In enacting this legislation, Congress noted the importance of access to television as a source of news, information, and entertainment for many Americans. This legislation demonstrates that the federal government intends for equal access to be a consideration in all aspects of daily life, including entertainment media.

The Telecommunications Act of 1996

The Telecommunications Act of 1996 establishes access requirements for telecommunications equipment and services, applying to the design, manufacture, and delivery of telecommunications services. Intended to promote both physical and intellectual access, this law instructs that, whenever possible, accessible telecommunications technology should be used for providing information and services at affordable rates (Kennard & Lyle, 2001). The Telecommunications Act of 1996's primary importance to access is in fostering the growth of information technology and services that are accessible for persons with disabilities. By promoting the creation and availability of accessible telecommunications technology, this act has a dual function in increasing accessibility. First, it promotes the growth of technologies, such as broadband, that open new possibilities for individuals with disabilities. For example, broadband has the potential to allow speakers of sign language to speak face-to-face in real time over long distances to communicate fully, including signing, lip reading, and reading of facial expressions. Second, by fostering the creation of more accessible technologies, the act has promoted the use of accessible technologies in other areas related to or reliant on telecommunications.

Section 508 of the Rehabilitation Act

One of the strongest elements of the mandate for access is Section 508 of the Rehabilitation Act. Section 508, which took effect in 2001, was created to address the extensive access problems that individuals with disabilities were encountering in federal government technology and the services provided using that technology. The act requires that members of the public with disabilities and government employees with disabilities have equal access to and use of information and communication technologies. Section 508 establishes accessibility requirements for software applications, operating systems, Web-based information and applications, telecommunications products, video and multimedia products, self-contained or closed products, desktop computers, and portable computers. Section 508 also prohibits covered entities from "developing, procuring, maintaining, or using" noncompliant information technology (29 U.S.C. § 794d(a)(1)(A–B)).

Section 508 does not apply directly to anything but federal government agencies and vendors who serve the federal government. However, organizations and state agencies that receive federal funding under certain funding programs are also required to comply with the requirements of Section 508. As a result, all state governments must comply with Section 508, "along with recipients of federal funds passed along" by the states (Boyer, 2000, p. 28). This law has the potential to greatly improve access to information technology for persons with disabilities. Federal employees with disabilities will have much greater access to technology at work, as will members of the public with disabilities.

ACCESS UNDER THE LAW: THE ACCESSIBILITY MANDATE

The combination of these laws establishes a mandate of access to most aspects of society for persons with disabilities. These laws establish rights of access, physical and intellectual, in many different aspects of society, including education, employment, public services, structures, commerce, information, and services. Some laws, such as the Architectural Barriers Act, relate exclusively to issues of physical access. However, the majority of the laws involve issues of both physical and intellectual access. The three primary laws that both classify disability and provide for access, Section 504 of the Rehabilitation Act, the ADA, and IDEA, all have components related to physical and intellectual access. Taken together, these laws demonstrate a clear intent by Congress to provide for equal physical and intellectual access to a wide range of aspects of society, including the online environment, for individuals with disabilities (Jaeger, 2004a, 2004b). As is discussed in chapter 7, however, equal access to the World Wide Web is still primarily a distant goal.

7

Accessibility and Technology in Application: Unequal Access Online

The amazingly rapid rise of the World Wide Web in the past decade has been nothing short of phenomenal. A technology that was basically unknown among the general public ten years ago is now considered an essential aspect of daily life by many people in the United States and in many other nations that have begun to evolve into information societies. The Internet, and associated features like e-mail, is a technology with great potential benefits for society and for the individual. "Although still in its adolescence, the core transformative capacities of the Internet include its potential for radically shrinking communications and information costs, maximizing speed, broadening reach, and eradicating distance" (Norris, 2001, p. 232). Access to the Web is far from universal at this point, however, as what has been termed the digital divide exists between those who have access to the Internet and those who do not.

The Internet was originally designed to be a text-only medium that could be read or converted to another format that would be accessible for all users. As such, the Internet was originally a fairly egalitarian medium for most users with disabilities. As the content of the Internet has become more popular and more complex, constantly evolving graphical, auditory, and other features have made it continually harder for persons with visual, hearing, mobility, cognitive, and learning disabilities to use the Web. Though assistive technologies and adaptive devices have been designed to help overcome the general inaccessibility of the online environment, so long as most sites are not developed to be accessible to users with disabilities, many of the services and much of the content on the Web remain beyond the reach of many persons with disabilities. Recognizing the importance of accessibility in the online environment, the World Wide Web Consortium began to develop the Web Content Accessibility Guidelines in the late 1990s. These guidelines are recommendations for all Web sites to follow to ensure accessibility for users with a range of disabilities, emphasizing design for full accessibility for all persons with disabilities in the creation of a Web site (World Wide Web Consortium, 1998).

Often, "the problems of Internet access are common to the problems of access to other communication and information technologies" (Norris, 2001, p. 66). Many of the services and activities available through the World Wide Web might be most useful to the people who may be least able to access them ("A Survey of Government," 2000). Tremendous gaps in availability of basic information technology exist in many areas of the world, both across national boundaries and within individual nations (Jaeger & Thompson, 2003; Yu, 2002). In access to and use of the Internet, major gaps in the U.S. population include economic, educational, racial, geographic, and disability gaps (Leslie Harris & Associates, 2002). Efforts have been made to provide computer access and training to members of these groups through public schools and public libraries (Department of Commerce, 2000). Residents of poorer communities or neighborhoods may be able to access online information in public facilities, "but this is not the same as having automatic access via high-speed connections at home and at the office" (Norris, 2001, p. 92). For persons with disabilities, however, the situation regarding limited usage of the Web results most directly from the limited accessibility of most Web sites and services on the Web.

This chapter examines disability and access to the online environment, giving special attention to access to electronic government for individuals with disabilities. Electronic government (e-government) is the provision of government information and services through the World Wide Web at the local, state, or national level. E-government, which has grown increasingly important in the United States and many other nations over the past few years, has the potential to alter citizen interactions with the government by promoting more active involvement in the political process. E-government, if implemented properly, can improve current government services, result in more accurate and efficient delivery of services, reduce administrative costs and time spent on repetitive tasks by government employees, facilitate greater accountability and transparency in the administration of government, and allow greater access to services due to the around-the-clock availability of the Web. Because most nations, as well as many state and local governments, are putting great efforts into creating viable e-governments, it is extremely important to make sure that the development of e-government accounts for the needs of individuals with disabilities. The failure to make e-government accessible threatens to lead to a virtual disenfranchisement of persons with disabilities (Jaeger, 2003b, 2004a, 2004b; Jaeger & Thompson, 2003, 2004).

DISABILITY RIGHTS IN CYBERSPACE

Persons with disabilities have some of the lowest levels of computer and Internet usage in the entire American population, as persons with disabilities are only half as likely to have Internet access (Department of Commerce, 2000). The number of persons with disabilities who have never used a computer is two and a half times greater than the number of nondisabled individuals who have never used a computer (Department of Commerce, 2000). This problem is not limited to the United States, as the European Union has identified a clear "disability gap" in access to information and communication technologies among its member nations (European Union, 2001, p. 11).

Part of these differences may be based on economics, as persons with disabilities typically have "far lower incomes than other citizens" (National Council on Disability, 2001, p. 103). As a number of studies have shown, income level certainly plays a powerful part in determining who can get online (Department of Commerce, 2002; Leslie Harris & Associates, 2002). However, the most significant reason for the lack of computer and Internet usage by persons with disabilities may be the prevalence of technological barriers. As computer technology has grown more sophisticated, "many changes that generally made it easier for non-disabled people to use computers often created barriers for people with disabilities" (Department of Justice, 2001, p. 1). Even if Web sites and other Internet technologies are made completely accessible, though, a significant percentage of individuals with disabilities do not have access to a computer and, therefore, have limited opportunities to ever reach the fully accessible Web sites.

> Cathy is a college sophomore who has enrolled in an online course in which the professor has decided to have interactions in the classroom and online. The instructor has set up a course Web site where students can access readings, get assignment instructions, and submit their completed assignments. The instructor also wants the class to engage in real-time discussions in a chat room on the course Web site, requiring each student to post at least two comments in each discussion.
>
> Being blind, Cathy relies on screen reader software to navigate the Web. The instructor failed to ensure that everything on the course Web site was accessible, so much of the content is incompatible with Cathy's screen reading program. To make matters worse, the screen reader cannot keep up with the pace of the online discussions, so she cannot post comments quickly enough. Mentioning these problems to her professor, Cathy was told that she obviously needed to buy better technology and that any issues were clearly her problem. Cathy had no choice but to drop the course.

As previously discussed, physical and intellectual access are essential for individuals with disabilities to achieve social equality. The federal government has passed a number of disability rights laws related to the accessibility of information technology, as discussed in chapter 6. The laws demonstrate progress toward ensuring some form of accessibility to technologies, and a number of these federal disability rights laws have application in cyberspace. Section 504 of the Rehabilitation Act, which covers the federal government and entities receiving federal funds, established the first standards of equal access to technology for individuals with disabilities. Many federal, state, and local government Web sites are funded, at least in part, by such federal monies.

The ADA prohibits discrimination against persons with disabilities by various private and public institutions. When it was passed in 1990, the ADA did not directly address issues related to the World Wide Web, as "cyberspace belonged to the realm of science fiction" (Bick, 2000, p. 225). However, by mandating that state and local governments equally include individuals with disabilities in all "services, programs, or activities of a public entity" (28 C.F.R. § 35.130), the ADA established that state and local government Web sites must be accessible to individuals with disabilities. There is a standing controversy as to whether commercial Web sites and Internet services are public accommodations under the meaning of the ADA (Bick, 2000; Konkright, 2001; Lane, 2002; Maroney, 2000; Petruzzelli, 2001; Ranen, 2002; Robertson, 2001; Schloss, 2001; Taylor, 2001). The cases that have been brought on the issue have resulted in court opinions with conflicting conclusions (*Access Now, Inc. v. Southwest Airlines*, 2002; *Rendon v. Valley Crest Productions*, 2002), though the Department of Justice has interpreted the ADA to apply to the Internet (National Council on Disability, 2001). The mandate of the ADA may well guarantee that Internet service providers be fully accessible, thus ensuring individuals with disabilities an equal ability to access the World Wide Web.

The Telecommunications Act of 1996 establishes accessibility require-ments for telecommunications equipment and services, applying to the de-sign, manufacture, and delivery of telecommunications services. Intended to provide both physical and intellectual access, this law mandates that, when possible, accessible telecommunications technology is available for federal agencies providing government information and services online (Kennard & Lyle, 2001).

The most comprehensive mandate for online accessibility is Section 508 of the Rehabilitation Act. Section 508 establishes accessibility requirements for government information and services involving technology; as such, any online content or services covered by Section 508 should be accessible to persons with disabilities. As the Internet is an information technology that is used both by the general public with disabilities and by government em-ployees with disabilities, Section 508 establishes that online government functions should be accessible. As existing Web sites are updated and new sites are brought online, Section 508 requires that the sites be accessible for persons with disabilities so that all citizens may use the sites equally.

ELECTRONIC GOVERNMENT AND DISABILITY

E-government employs "technology, particularly the Internet, to enhance the access to and delivery of government information and services to citizens, businesses, government employees, and other agencies" at the federal, state, and local levels (Hernon, Reylea, Dugan, & Cheverie, 2002, p. 388). E-government provides citizens with the opportunity to have a greater voice in governance, to receive more efficient and effective services, and to be "more informed about government laws, regulations, policies, and services" (Muir & Oppenheim, 2002a, p. 175). E-government has the potential to allow the government to "connect directly with its citizens and enhance service delivery, provide sustainable economic development, and safeguard democracy" (Toregas, 2001, p. 235). The E-government Act of 2002 is intended to expand the involvement of citizens, including individuals with disabilities. E-government is having an impact on several areas of democracy in many nations, including access to political information, communication about political issues, communication with government officials and elected representatives, and delivery of government services. These processes, if fully accessible, could eradicate many of the barriers persons with disabilities have previously faced in the operation of the government.

Many people go online to become involved in civic matters, engage public officials, research public policy issues, gather information to cast votes, participate in online lobbying campaigns, and take part in numerous other activities related to citizenship (Larsen & Rainie, 2002). In the United States, almost two of every three online adults have used e-government information or services at least once (National Information Center, 2000), while nearly one third of Internet users identify the use of e-government as a regular part of their online activities (Department of Commerce, 2002). Nearly 60 percent of Internet users in the United States feel e-government is the best source for government information, and about two thirds of Americans expect that information they are seeking will be on a government Web site (Horrigan & Rainie, 2002). "More Americans have visited government Web sites than have sought financial information online, made travel reservations, sent instant messages, or gotten sports scores online" (Larsen & Rainie, 2002, p. 5).

Individuals with certain types of disabilities, such as vision and hearing impairments, learning disabilities, and mobility impairments, are still completely vulnerable to discrimination when e-government sites are not fully accessible. "While the number of e-government initiatives at the federal and state level continue to expand, access for the disabled is moving at a snail's

pace" (Newcombe, 2001, p. 25). If e-government information and services
are not fully accessible to persons with disabilities, then e-government is not
fulfilling the promise of a discrimination-free government (Jaeger, 2003a,
2004a, 2004b; Jaeger & Thompson, 2003, 2004). At this point, the federal
e-government is not successfully providing, much less guaranteeing, physical
and intellectual access for persons with disabilities.

THE IMPACT OF LAWS ON ONLINE ACCESSIBILITY

Before the passage of Section 508, federal agencies "did not focus on the
extent to which their mainstream technology was accessible to persons with
disabilities" (Department of Justice, 2001, p. 1). The effectiveness of accessibility laws will hinge on how well they are implemented, and the results
thus far are not encouraging. One study reviewed 148 federal Web sites and
found that only 13.5 percent were accessible (Stowers, 2002). A further study
found 28 percent of the Web sites to have accessibility features (West,
2002a), while yet another study found that only 22 percent of federal Web
sites were in compliance with Section 508 requirements (West, 2003). Overall, most major government agencies have significant accessibility problems in
their Web sites (Ellison, 2004). Accessibility is even a problem on the First-
Gov Web site, which is the official portal for e-government in the United
States (Jaeger, 2004a; Michael, 2004). In spite of these low levels of accessibility, however, the United States has so far put greater effort than any other
nation into promoting accessibility in e-government (Muir & Oppenheim,
2002b).

In fact, a 2001 study comparing e-governments around the world
found that accessibility was virtually nonexistent on the vast majority of e-
government sites (World Markets Research Centre). In the years since 2001,
accessibility has not developed as a priority in many of these nations. Even
nations that are attempting to improve the accessibility of e-government
sites are not necessarily succeeding. A 2004 study of 1,000 e-government
sites in the United Kingdom found 81 percent had significant accessibility
problems (Disability Rights Commission). Serious accessibility problems
have been identified in the government Web sites of many other members of
the European Union, such as Denmark, France, and Ireland (Marincu &
McMullin, 2004).

A fear of cost has contributed to resistance to the implementation of accessibility on e-government sites. In the United States, some agencies have
argued against compliance with Section 508 as a waste of money, talent, and
time, while other agencies have only made a limited number of Web pages
accessible (Lais, 2000; McLawhorn, 2001; Thibodeau, 2001). The United
States is the world's largest spender on e-government (Booz Allen Hamilton,
2002), yet funding for accessibility is scarce. As a result, some agencies have
even rewritten contracts in an attempt to force all responsibility for Section

508 on their vendors (Matthews, 2001a). However, "the costs of doing nothing may be greater than the costs of any reasonably foreseeable measures" (National Council on Disability, 2001, p. 28).

Cost is not the only impediment to accessibility. The Web sites of some agencies that have been modified in an attempt to comply with Section 508 display scant understanding of the law and what it requires. Some agencies apparently never understood when they had to be in compliance (Tang, 2001), while many other federal Web sites were suspended or shut down permanently to avoid having to comply (McLawhorn, 2001). Certain parts of the government have proclaimed their Web sites fully accessible, only to find that their sites were in fact riddled with accessibility problems (Matthews, 2001b, 2002). In some cases in the private and public sectors, organizations or their Web site developers simply do not care about issues of accessibility. A recent study of Web masters for government and commercial organizations found that many "would only make web sites accessible if the government forced them to" (Lazar, Dudley-Sponaugle, & Greenidge, 2004, p. 284). The same study found most respondents were unaware of how to make their sites accessible, had limited understanding of what was required or where to find more information, and were generally disinterested in accessibility or potential users with disabilities.

More hopefully, Section 508 appears to have inspired a number of state and local governments to "look at accessibility as a genuine opportunity to bring government resources and services to an increasing number of people" (Patterson, 2002, p. 10). Many local government agencies "are getting ahead of the game by making their online information and services available in universally accessible formats" when they are first made available online (Williams, 2001, p. 12). A 2002 study of the accessibility of state e-government sites found Connecticut to have the most accessible sites, with an admirable 92 percent of sites being accessible (West, 2002a). The only other states with more than half of e-government sites being accessible, however, were North Dakota (58 percent), Oregon (58 percent), Pennsylvania (56 percent), and Montana (52 percent) (West, 2002a). Other studies of state government Web sites have found accessibility problems are widespread on most sites (Fagan & Fagan, 2004). Another study issued in September 2002 found "a dramatic increase in disability access" in local e-governments, revealing that 82 percent of local e-government sites offered some kind of accessibility features (West, 2002b, pp. 7–8).

Another encouraging fact is that a much greater number of federal government Web sites than commercial Web sites are accessible. Even though full accessibility can dramatically increase the usage of a site, few commercial sites have actually become accessible unless threatened with a lawsuit (Gibson, 2001). A 2002 study found that a disheartening 1.76 percent of commercial Web sites it examined (19 out of 1,080) were actually accessible (Milliman, 2002). These commercial organizations indicated an array of reasons for not addressing issues of accessibility, including the lack of demonstrated benefits for the business, the cost, the absence of legal penalties, and unawareness of how to make a site accessible (Milliman, 2002).

ACCESS IN THE INFORMATION AGE

As information and communication technologies continue to become more important in everyday life, equal access to ICTs will continue to grow in significance. Ensuring access to technology is an unending task, as equal access must be gained each time a new ICT comes to prominence. Preserving access to established entities is a continual effort as well. Even though accessible buildings have been becoming more commonplace over the past three decades, not all buildings are fully accessible for every person with a disability. The longest battles for equal access—to education, to employment, to government, to physical structures—seem likely to continue. Things may become more accessible, but issues of access will always be a part of the life of each person with a disability.

The interrelationships between classifications and levels of socially guaranteed access explored in part II reveal the myriad ways in which different social issues related to disability can be entwined. Part III explores representation of disability, a further issue that is tied to classification and access. The ways in which disability is represented across media are linked to the social classifications of disability and the levels of access persons with disabilities have to those media and to society as a whole.

III

Social Representations
of Disability

8

The Social Significance of the Representation of Disability

"The cultural representation of people with disabilities affects our understanding of what it means to be human; in more practical terms, it affects public policy, the allocation of social resources, and the meaning of civil rights" (Berube, 1997, pp. B4–B5). Representations of disability are made by people who have disabilities and by people who do not. For persons with disabilities, these representations stem from their experiences as persons with disability and as significant others, friends, family members, and/or caregivers. Sometimes the experience of some aspect of living with disability is the subject of literature, music, or visual arts. The work of art may focus on the experience of acquiring a changed identity (getting sick, getting an injury, etc.) or the experience of moving with a familiar but "different" identity into a new life experience (puberty, a new job, a new living situation, or new relationships). Sometimes the experience of some aspect of living with disability is incorporated as part of the life experience and circumstances that are either central or peripheral for the character who may be either central or peripheral to the work of art.

I had a student teacher, a beautiful and vivacious young woman with a passion for teaching, in my senior English class. She had been in a serious automobile accident at the age of 16 and subsequently needed a wheelchair for mobility. She did a beautiful job, and, with the presence of a veteran teacher, kept the class engaged in reading and writing activities. The boys in the class responded to her more quickly than the girls. After the end of her semester with us, I asked my students about their personal reactions to her. The boys immediately noted her appearance, her sense of humor, and her willingness to try new activities. The girls responded more reflectively, focusing on her abilities as a teacher. As they struggled to explain, one girl said, "I just kept thinking that she is only five years older than I am and it could have been me in that wheelchair."

Representations of disability can be a vehicle for broader social fears or needs, such as the effects of industrialization, the expression of evil, or the potential healing power of charity (Shakespeare, 1994). Representations of disability can be, and are often intended to be, very upsetting because they make people question their own health and mortality. "No one is ever more than temporarily able-bodied" (Breckenridge & Vogler, 2001, p. 349).

Attitudes and policies that deny basic human rights and equal opportunities to people with disabilities are evident in education, employment, the benefit system, support services, the built environment, the leisure industry, and the media. Stereotyped assumptions about persons with disabilities are often based on superstition, myths, and beliefs from earlier, less enlightened times. They are inherent to our culture and persist partly because they are constantly reproduced through the media. Many of the classifications of persons with disabilities, discussed earlier in this book, are perpetuated by representations in the media through a number of different means.

REPRESENTATION

Representation is applied in different ways according to the occasion of its use and is a potent concept as a whole, especially for a minority that can be seen to be underrepresented in society. Richard Dyer (1988) identified four senses of representation. Each of the senses he spoke about has relevance in the study of portrayals of persons with disabilities.

The first sense he called "re-presenting"; how media re-presents our world to us. Representation insists that there is a real world, but that our perception of it is always mediated by the media's selection, emphasis, and use of technical/aesthetic means to render that world to us (Dyer, 1988).

The second sense identified by Dyer is that of being representative of something—being a typicality. To what extent are the portrayals of women, the gay community, or persons with disabilities typical of how those groups manifest themselves in society? Dyer maintained that we cannot communicate the individuated or the unique; we must always deal with the typical.

The third sense of representation referred to is that of representation as speaking for people. Faced with media images, we constantly need to ask, "Who is speaking here?" This applies mostly, according to Dyer, for groups outside the mainstream of speech. For those people with disabilities who for a century have existed in Norden's (1994) "cinema of isolation," it has been directors, writers, and actors without disabilities who have spoken on their behalf.

The final sense of representation identified by Dyer asks the question, "What does the image represent to the people who are watching?" This is not necessarily always the same as its "ideal" meaning or that intended by those who produced it.

As society's attitudes change, media will reflect those attitudes. However, media can also play an active role in challenging society's fear and misunderstanding of disability by consciously seeking to portray characters with disabilities realistically, fairly and frequently. Providing realistic portrayals of disability will help in both the construction of a healthy self-image for persons with disabilities and a more informed image for those who never come in close personal contact with individuals with disabilities.

Ultimately, representations of disability in a work reveal the attitudes about disability that the author believes to be socially acceptable. Many negative representations of disability result from bias by the creator, even if the creator is familiar with the issues related to disability. For example, Virginia Woolf, even though she had a sister who lived in an institution, wrote very disparaging comments about persons with disabilities in her diary (Lee, 1997).

NEGATIVE CULTURAL STEREOTYPES

The link between the representation of impairment and all that is socially unacceptable has origins in classical Greek theatre. Today a number of cultural stereotypes perpetuate this linkage. This is particularly the case with fictional characterizations. Evil, for example, is often combined with sexual degeneracy in the characterization of persons with disabilities. The seven most common modern representations of persons with disabilities across media include: pitiful and pathetic; supercrip; sinister, evil, and criminal; better off dead; maladjusted and their own worst enemy; burden; and unable to live a successful life (Biklen & Bogdan, 1982). The point is that the overall representation of persons with disabilities is decidedly negative and conveys a threat to the rest of society.

This predominantly negative view of persons with disabilities appears regularly in the news media both on television and in the press (Ennes & Smit, 2001; Pointon & Davis, 1997). Pictures of individuals with disabilities, frequently children, in hospitals or nursing homes are repeatedly flashed across our television screens perpetuating the myth that disability is synonymous with illness and suffering. Many reports about persons with disabilities in television news programs and documentaries are about medical treatments and impairment-related cures. Persons with disabilities are sometimes included in the storylines of films and television dramas to enhance a certain atmosphere, usually one of menace, mystery, or deprivation, or to add character to the visual impact of the production (Black, 2004; Longmore, 1987, 2003; Norden, 1994). This dilutes the humanity of persons with disabilities by reducing them to objects of curiosity.

Media oftentimes represent persons with disabilities as self-pitying individuals who could overcome their difficulties if they would stop feeling sorry for themselves, think positively, and rise to the challenge. This is a recurrent theme in many films that document the psychological trauma of coming to terms with disability in society (Black, 2004; Longmore, 1987, 2003). Often the hero is saved by a heterosexual relationship, which is probably a positive step since movies have historically represented people with disabilities as sexually inactive. Such views stem directly from the traditional medical view of disability. The individual assumptions at the heart of this approach lead to a psychology of impairment that interprets the behavior of persons with disabilities as individual pathology. It allows society to reinterpret legitimate anger or frustration related to the challenges of a disability as self-destructive bitterness arising out of an inability to accept the limitations of impairment.

ACTS OF CHARITY?

"To be seen as a patient or in need of charity is to be thought incapable of the same life as others. To be lauded for super-achievement is to suggest that a disabled person can turn our pity into respect only at the point of having accomplished some extraordinary feat" (Shapiro, 1994, p. 124). Telethons and infomercials encourage pity so that the nondisabled public can feel bountiful (Charlton, 1998). It is a regular feature of popular fiction; overtly dependent persons with disabilities are included in storylines to depict another character's goodness and sensitivity (Black, 2004). The person with a disability is frequently portrayed as especially endearing to elicit even greater feelings of sentimentality as opposed to genuine compassion. A telling example includes Porgy in George Gershwin's opera *Porgy and Bess*. Likewise, poster children are often selected to tug at the heartstrings of society for donations and other gifts.

The individual with a disability, oftentimes, is assigned superhuman, almost magical abilities. Blind people are frequently portrayed as visionaries with a sixth sense or extremely sensitive hearing. Alternatively, individuals with disabilities, especially children, are praised excessively for relatively ordinary achievements. In the award-winning film, *My Left Foot*, we learn how Christy Brown overcame both impairment and the poverty of working-class life in Dublin in the 1930s to become nationally acclaimed as an artist, writer, and poet. The film was based on his autobiography. It is notable that although this film provided an excellent opportunity for an actor with a disability to play Brown, Daniel Day Lewis, who has no disability, played the role.

SEXUALITY AND DISABILITY

Misguided presumptions about the sexuality of persons with disabilities have been a common theme in literature and art since ancient times.

Moreover, the vast majority of these images are about male experiences—there has been little if any exploration of the sexuality of women with disabilities. For example, in Homer's *Odyssey* (approximately 500 BCE), Odysseus is entertained in the Phaecian palace of Alcinous by Denodecus's tale of Aphrodite's adulterous affair with Ares because her husband Hephaestus is a "cripple." Until recently, persons with disabilities have, with few exceptions, been represented as incapable of sexual activity. A more recent example is D. H. Lawrence's (2001) novel *Lady Chatterley's Lover* (first published in 1928), a book about an affair between Lady Chatterley and a gamekeeper, Meadows. The relationship takes place because Lady Chatterley's husband has a disability and is perceived by Lawrence as sexually inactive; this assumption has been labeled "the Chatterley syndrome" by one literary critic (Battye, 1966). This assumption is so widespread that examples can be found in pop music, films, television, and the press. Country and western singer Kenny Rogers had a worldwide hit with the song "Ruby, Don't Take Your Love to Town." The song's lyrics tell the story of a war veteran begging his lover, Ruby, not to let a war injury that affected the physical side of their relationship come between them.

VIOLENCE AND DISABILITY

Persons with disabilities are often subject to violent abuse, and this is frequently reflected in the media. Besides contributing to and underlining the mistaken belief that persons with disabilities are totally helpless and dependent, such imagery helps perpetuate this violence. As detailed in chapter 3, persons with disabilities have been the victims of oppression and violence throughout recorded history. The ancient Greeks and Romans were advocates of infanticide for children with disabilities. In medieval Europe, disability was associated with evil and witchcraft. In some areas, religious leaders approved the persecution and murder of disabled people. For example, Martin Luther, the Protestant reformer, said he saw evil in children with disabilities. Since the industrial revolution, similar practices have been sanctioned by science and, to some extent, the media.

A surprising modern forum for the representation of disability in relation to violence can be found in wrestling. The spectacle of wrestling has a grip on more than advertising dollars. It also exerts a great deal of social influence through the messages it delivers in its storylines and stereotypes. Wrestling works as a part of television in general to effectively mold viewer attitudes (Nelson, 1996). Thus, it is believed that viewers look to television and other mass media for cues about social reality and for education about dealing with the social situations that they encounter (Wahl, 1995). Stereotypes are an integral part of wrestling's appeal; few other rituals in American culture equal wrestling in its range of symbols and stereotypes (Ball, 1990). In this context, wrestling has often been characterized as an explicitly dramatic form of entertainment—comparable to the soap opera (Mondak, 1989). No other modern public event better demonstrates the social influence of wrestling than the 1998 election of Jesse Ventura, a former professional wrestler with little political experience, as Minnesota governor. Indeed, wrestling, as a popular example of media sources, is a specific influence on people's ideas about many social phenomena, including mental illness and mental disabilities.

The stereotype of the mentally ill professional wrestler is a relatively recent one, although in many ways its prototype has been part of the spectacle for decades (Ball, 1990). Wrestling, which has ancient roots and has cycled in and out of popularity since the early 1900s, has traditionally embraced a "freak show" element to attract fans. Since the mass media are powerful in shaping attitudes toward people with mental illness or mental disabilities, the messages sent through programs like wrestling have an impact on the classifications of, and reactions to, disability. Because professional wrestling is an extremely popular form of entertainment, especially for young, often impressionable viewers, understanding the messages it presents about any group is necessary.

THE VALUE OF MORE HONEST PORTRAYALS

How someone with a disability is represented in the mass media can have a powerful effect on people. Much of what we know of people, places, and events comes from what we see on television and in movies or read in the papers. Currently in film and television, persons with disabilities are primarily portrayed stereotypically, characters created by someone with little knowledge of the attitudes and abilities of an individual with a disability (Black, 2004; Longmore, 1987, 2003; Norden, 1994). Several modern television shows, however, portray disability in a more realistic manner, including *Joan of Arcadia, The West Wing, Ed, House,* and several daytime soap operas.

While representations in the media perpetuate stereotyped notions of persons with disabilities, the media may also be the best path to encouraging true understanding. More and more actors with disabilities are appearing in commercials and roles in the mainstream media. Some of these characters with disabilities are much better written and not so much "about the disability." It is up to actors, artists, musicians, writers, producers, and directors with disabilities to work toward better and more abundant representation across different media.

A person with a disability has the potential to present a provocative image, and the choice to use such a character provides a powerful tool for the dramatic narrative. Unfortunately, representations of disability in the media often unintentionally perpetuate stereotypes through characters with disabilities being portrayed to evoke pity, bitterness, or unhappiness, or as inspirational heroes. But perhaps the most significant advances in the mass media portrayal of people with disabilities come from advertisers who see these people as something much more than having a disability; they are seen as consumers. Ads that represent people with disabilities playing sports, shopping, teaching, driving, and eating at McDonald's make society aware that people with disabilities do the same things everyone else does.

Specialized resources are now available to help promote positive representations of persons with disabilities. The National Arts and Disability Center (NADC) is the national information dissemination, technical assistance, and referral center specializing in the field of arts and disability. Dedicated to promoting the full inclusion of children and adults with disabilities in the visual, performing, media, and literary arts communities, the NADC serves to advance artists with disabilities and accessibility to the arts. Its Web site, http://nadc.ucla.edu, provides access to its resource directories, annotated bibliographies, and conferences.

9

Representations of Disability across Media

Disability has been represented in art for thousands of years, and the study and teaching of those representations of disability in historical context has the potential to raise awareness and understanding of disability as a cultural issue. This increased awareness may help place disability in the continuum of diversity issues, rather than being frequently ignored.

Tiny Tim, Captain Hook, and Helen Keller are three seemingly unrelated figures found in popular literature. The first two are fictional characters, while the real life story of Helen Keller has been portrayed many times. They do have a prominent common characteristic: a disability. Tiny Tim has brought tears to the eyes of readers and movie goers as he faced the adversity of hobbling around on crutches at such a tender age while enthusiastically exclaiming, "God bless us everyone!" We have scorned that bitter, scheming captain with a hook for a hand as he attempted to bring about the demise of the ever-magical boy in green tights. The biographical story of Helen Keller has inspired many people who watched her face deafness, blindness, and underestimation on her way to brilliance. If you let these three literary figures swirl in your brain for a minute, you just might be able to relive the heartbreaking innocence and irony of Tiny Tim's blessing, the deep hatred for the despicable Captain Hook, and the feeling of general good as Helen Keller finally achieved the fame she so richly deserved. What you likely will not realize is the typical stereotypes that these literary figures fulfill and have been fulfilling in the media for decades on end—disabled innocence (Tiny Tim), disabled evil (Captain Hook), and disabled inspiration (Helen Keller).

The representation of persons with disabilities in literature and mass media has been varied and often negative. Inappropriate portrayals have engendered attitudes ranging from feelings of pity or revulsion to expectations of superhuman powers of intellect or insight. When disability is represented artistically, it can be based on stereotypes, on imagination, on personal experience as a person with a disability, or on the experiences of friends, family members, or caregivers with disabilities.

LITERATURE AND DISABILITY

In literature, disability may be incorporated as part of the life experiences that are either central or peripheral for the character in the work. Often, the disability functions as a marker, the character so designated as a foil or a representative of weakness and evil or unearthly purity, pathos, spirituality, and self-abnegation. This emphasis on the impairment is often reflected in how disability is portrayed. Literature about disability appears in every cultural medium, genre, and subgenre and has been treated from every possible perspective–as stigma, divine challenge, divine punishment, defeat, part of everyday life, and as opportunity or challenge. In representing those with disabilities, writers often veer between competing impulses toward hagiography and demonization.

Literary representations of disability tend to emphasize the otherness of disability and the exclusion of characters with disabilities (Bowman & Jaeger, 2003, 2004; Thomson, 1997). In literature, the disabled body is a "repository for social anxiety about such troubling concerns as vulnerability, control, and identity" (Thomson, 1997, p. 6). Varying cultural meanings of disability have reflected historical and social contexts. For example, in much postapocalyptic science fiction, those disabled or born mutated because of radiation exposure are most often represented as the enemies, the "others," the source of conflict or danger to be overcome by the survivors. They are the "bad guys," similar to the deformed and crippled king in Shakespeare's *Richard III* (first performed in 1597). A few examples of well-known literary texts with representations of a disability that dominate the text include the following.

In Sophocles's *Oedipus Rex* (first performed in approximately 430 BCE), Laius, ruler of Thebes, is told by an oracle that his son will kill him. With the agreement of his wife, Jocasta, the baby's feet are pinioned and he is given to a slave to be exposed on nearby Mt. Cithaeron, a haunt of wolves and other wild beasts. The slave, a shepherd of Laius's flocks, takes pity on the baby, and instead of leaving it to die gives the boy to a fellow shepherd from Corinth, on the other side of the mountain. The Corinthian shepherd presents the baby to the childless king of Corinth, Polybus, who brings him up as his own, presumably giving him the name Oedipus (Swollen Foot) because of his deformity.

In the essay "Of a Monstrous Child" (first published in approximately 1580), Montaigne (1958) describes two children joined together at birth in a heartbreakingly graphic manner and the family who planned to capitalize on this strangeness for financial gain by making the children beggars. "Under his paps he was fastned and joyned to another childe, but had no head, and who had the conduite of his backe stopped; the rest whole. One of his armes was shorter than the other, and was by accident broken at their birth. They were joyned face to face, and as if a little child would embrace another somewhat bigger" (spelling as in original, pp. 538–539).

In Francis Bacon's (1985) "Of Deformity" (first published in 1625), the author struggled with the causes and effects of disability:

> Deformed persons are commonly even with nature; for as nature hath done ill by them, so do they by nature; being for the most part (as the Scripture saith) void of natural affection; and so they have their revenge of nature.... Therefore it is good to consider of deformity, not as a sign, which is more deceivable; but as a cause, which seldom faileth of the effect. Whosoever hath anything fixed in his person, that doth induce contempt, hath also a perpetual spur in himself, to rescue and deliver himself from scorn. Therefore all deformed persons, are extreme bold.... So that upon the matter, in a great wit, deformity is an advantage to rising.... Still the ground is, they will, if they be of spirit, seek to free themselves from scorn; which must be either by virtue or malice; and therefore let it not be marvelled, if sometimes they prove excellent persons. (pp. 191–192)

In Herman Melville's (1987) *Moby Dick* (first published in 1851), Captain Ahab becomes so obsessed by the white whale's destruction of one of his legs that he sacrifices himself and most of his crew in pursuit of revenge. Melville uses impairment to heighten the sinister atmosphere of the book, as narrator Ishmael describes Ahab's false leg tapping back and forth across the deck in the middle of the night.

DISABILITY DOESN'T SELL

It is a simple task to find many criticisms of the representation of disability in television and film (Black, 2004; Longmore, 2003; Norden, 1994), as well as in journalism (Black, 2004; Ennes & Smit, 2001; Norden, 1994; Pointon & Davies, 1997) and photography (Hervey, 1992). Representations of disability on television are almost invariably either negative stereotypes or stories that romanticize disability and make it the heroic story of overcoming the odds, creating images of "supercrips" (Ware, 2002).

In television and movies, the common portrayal of persons with disabilities as villains or monsters reinforces three common stereotypes: disability as punishment, disability causing bitterness, and disability causing resentment of others. These portrayals also link disability to a loss of humanity (Longmore,

2003). Typically, characters with disabilities are less accepting of their disabilities than are those around them, except for the characters with disabilities who have overcome their impairments and have achieved special gifts as a result. Positive and realistic images of disability in visual media are most frequent in commercials, where advertisers recognize persons with disabilities as a potential market for their products (Longmore, 2003).

Much filmmaking follows a formula. If a film makes money, it is deemed a success. It will make more money if an established star plays the lead. Somebody attractive who at the end of the day can stand up from the wheelchair, remove the makeup, or shrug off the facial tics and gestures that indicated just how deeply immersed he or she was in the portrayal. We can read the interviews where the actor reveals a newfound empathy, dedicates the inevitable award to a particular cause, and becomes a spokesperson for a fashionable charity. It is the perfect partnership—the studios get to make a film with a popular actor drawing crowds, the celebrities get to flex their acting muscles, the critics respond accordingly, and everybody involved wins. *A Beautiful Mind* took in $170,708,996 at the box office, won four out of its five Golden Globe nominations, and four out of its eight Academy Award nominations. *Born on the Fourth of July* made $70,001,698, was nominated for eight Oscars and won two, also winning six of its seven Golden Globe nominations. *Rain Man* won four of its eight Oscar nominations and two out of its six Golden Globe nominations, and made $172,825,435 at the box office. Such financial and critical success, however, does not guarantee accurate representations of the disabilities that are so central to the films.

If high-profile, award-winning movies were to provide accurate, positive, and representative portrayals, could they increase awareness of individual abilities and social barriers encountered daily by people with disabilities? Some people believe that the best way to address the historically negative perceptions of disability is through examples of inclusion. Indeed, a large number of disability organizations focus on such a move, hoping to shrug off the notions of "handicapped" people who constantly rely on the charity of others. It would be wonderful to think that non-plot-driven representations of disability are addressing the problems of perception, but there is always the potential for tokenism to come into play, for producers to address a perceived politically correct agenda and only create stereotypes. Any minority representation has had to suffer similar setbacks in trying to achieve integration in the media. Take any 1970s situation comedy and you will most likely find some horribly stereotyped character. For many persons with disabilities, adversity comes in a variety of forms, most of which have to be accommodated and accepted rather than defiantly fought against. Public perception is just one of the barriers to civil rights and integration. Hollywood, with its formula, seems to want to portray persons with disabilities as fulfilling one of the following categories: exceptional, heartbreaking, comedic, or villainous (Black, 2004; Longmore, 1987, 2003).

The makers of movies that portray disability often fail to consider the needs of persons with disabilities even in advertising and promoting their movies. In *Daredevil*, Ben Affleck played a visually impaired lawyer, blinded by biochemical waste, but given superenhanced senses as some sort of cosmic payoff. If you want to find out more about *Daredevil*, visit the Web site at www.daredevilthemovie.com. If you are visually impaired, your screen reader will not likely be able to navigate the Flash-animated site, but it looks great. Similarly, *Children of a Lesser God*, one of the few films acclaimed for actually using an actor with a disability in a leading role (and winning her an Oscar as an added bonus) was shot in such a way that people with hearing impairments cannot read much of the sign language used throughout.

IS DISABILITY NEWS?

Accounts of disability in media are often informed only by medical and psychological perspectives, if they are informed at all (Ware, 2002). News stories related to disability usually focus on medical or technological innovations that will neutralize disabilities (Longmore, 2003). The problems with news media coverage of disability led disability rights activists to avoid courting media coverage when the ADA was being passed to prevent coverage that was unhelpful or negative (Shapiro, 1994). News media representations of disability tend to:

- Focus on the lawsuits and whether people actually have disabilities
- Emphasize cases where the claim lacks merit or the person has an "undeserving" disability
- Perpetuate the myth that if it is a common condition, it should not be considered a disability
- Portray disability rights laws as a problem
- View all disability issues in terms of "fairness" rather than civil rights (Lacheen, 2000)

As a whole, news representations tend to be negative toward persons with disabilities. By placing most of the emphasis on representing disability as a legal and social problem that makes life more difficult for others or on representing persons with disabilities as being undeserving, the news media coverage of disability mainly serves to make life more difficult for persons with disabilities. These most common representations also reveal a lack of awareness about persons with disabilities and the issues they face. Such representations could be more balanced with further research and consultation with national and international disability organizations, local disability organizations, and individuals with disabilities themselves.

REPRESENTATIONS OF DISABILITY BY PERSONS
WITH DISABILITIES

For much of human history, people with disabilities were not the creators
of representations of disabilities. However, representations of disability by
persons with disabilities can produce much more honest and realistic portrayals of, and insights into, disability. Disability narratives offer "unnatural
histories, visions of lives lived against the grain of normalcy" (Rapp &
Ginsburg, 2001, p. 552). Frequently, artists with disabilities convey much
about finding meaning about disability on a personal level.

John Milton (1961), in "On His Blindness" (first published in approximately 1660) wrote:

> When I consider how my light is spent
> Ere half my days in this dark world and wide,
> And that one Talent which is death to hide
> Lodged with me useless, ... (1936, p. 613)

Milton struggled with the onset of blindness, questioning his self-worth as he
lost his ability to see his words on paper and seeking patience to endure.

In *The Autobiography of a Face* (first published in 1994), poet Lucy Grealy
(2003) tells the true story of her childhood and young adulthood, a twenty-
year period of overwhelming physical and mental suffering. At age nine, first
misdiagnosed and finally identified as having facial bone cancer (Ewing's
sarcoma), Lucy underwent several surgeries and more than two years of in-
tensive chemotherapy and radiation treatments. Pain and nausea, anxiety and
fear of more pain and nausea were only part of the ordeal. Lucy became aware
of what it is to be severely, chronically ill. Her sisters behaved differently
toward her. Being at home was worse than being in the hospital. There she felt
no guilt or shame; however, amid her family, she blamed herself for the ten-
sion, arguments over money, and her mother's depression. Her hair fell out
and she became aware that people were staring at her face. At school, Lucy's
disfigured face drew taunts from classmates; she understood that she was
perceived as ugly. Her moods alternated between despair, determination, and
escapism. She became convinced that only facial reconstruction and a restored
appearance would make life bearable. During years of reconstructive surgery,
Lucy evolved complex rationalizations to give meaning to her suffering. Two
anchors had stabilized her existence throughout the misery: a passionate
adolescent love of horses and an adult love of poetry. Eventually, outward
appearance and inner life became harmonious.

This story reveals much about the inner struggles of and external challenges for children with disabilities. Grealy addresses many of the topics hit
upon by other representations already discussed herein: exclusion, shunning
as a result of appearance, placement in facilities away from others, alienation

in education, and the stress of disability on the family. Though Grealy shows a range of negative representations of disability, the fact that she ultimately learns to live a successful and happy life demonstrates much positive, too. As people with disabilities strive for more accurate representations of life with a disability, they are beginning to examine in greater depth how they are represented and viewed in many different aspects of society.

10

"Nothing About Us without Us"

To understand a culture is to learn about its history and to hear about the effects of that history. To learn about a culture is to learn about class, gender relations, treatment of minority groups, and many other issues. To understand a culture requires talking with people from that culture about class, gender, and other issues. Learning about a culture calls for experiencing its poetry and its music, its pottery and its paintings. Understanding a culture means reading its literature and watching its movies. To understand a culture requires talking with people with disability from that culture about their experiences. Representations of disability are central to shaping the place and perception of persons with disabilities within society.

Media and popular culture interpret human events in artistic or analytical ways. Ever since human beings' earliest attempts to sketch pictures and manipulate language to describe the world around us, we have created cultural representations. As tools of communication became more sophisticated and reached wider audiences, words and images came to exert an even more powerful influence upon societies. Media and popular culture—such as books, movies, music, plays, television, magazines, and newspapers—became an important source of knowledge and insight about important human issues.

In the last two decades, disability rights groups around the world have begun to use the phrase "nothing about us without us" as a rallying cry. This phrase is meant to convey that persons with disabilities want to have a greater role in society and that "they know what is best for themselves and their community" (Charlton, 1998, p. 4). This attitude demonstrates a greater desire to participate not only in decisions affecting their own lives, but in social issues that affect them as a group. A key element of the latter involves beginning to analyze how persons with disabilities are represented in society and working to move those perceptions in a more positive direction. Such work is a tremendous task, because once you start thinking about it, disability is represented in some way in almost every facet of human existence. This chapter presents a sampling of the diverse contexts in which disability can be presented.

DISABILITY AND COMEDY

Laughing at disability is not new; persons with disabilities have been a source of amusement for nondisabled people for centuries, as evidenced by freak shows and markets for slaves with disabilities. Elizabethan-era jokes focused on people with every type of impairment imaginable. During the seventeenth and eighteenth centuries, keeping "idiots" as objects of humor was common among those who had the money to do so, and visits to Bedlam and other mental institutions were a typical form of entertainment for the "able but ignorant."

While such thoughtless behavior might be expected in earlier, less enlightened times, making fun of persons with disabilities may be as prevalent now as it was then. It is especially common among professional nondisabled comedians. Several of the comedy greats who influenced today's comedians built their careers around disablist humor. Harpo Marx, for example, pretended he could not speak to act the fool, and radio stars of the 1950s and early 1960s such as Al Read and Hilda Baker mocked their respective stooges by shouting at them as if they were deaf, and, by implication, stupid. There is a tremendous difference between mocking someone based on having a disability and finding humor in the everyday occurrences related to disability.

Life with a disability is often full of comical moments. Why not laugh when a wheelchair gets a flat tire? When someone looks closely to see how to use profanity in American Sign Language? When you see someone pointing to a person with a visual impairment? If disability was understood and recognized as a common aspect of human diversity, everyone could see the humor, not the tragedy, in these situations. We might find some commonalities across the margins to bring us together in diversity. We need to provide the kind of information and imagery that acknowledges and explores the complexity of the experience of disability and its relation to identity and that facilitates the meaningful integration of all persons with disabilities into the mainstream economic and social life of the community.

DISABILITY AND RELIGION

Learning about a culture is also learning about the role religion plays in a culture. Religions and belief systems are powerful shapers of culture, and many habits, customs, folktales, stereotypes, hopes, and fears of a community arise from the religious beliefs of that community. To discount the influence of religion on a culture is to forget an essential part of that culture. While religions play a larger role in some cultures than in others, religion is one of the greatest influences on any aspects of most cultures.

As with culture, religions and belief systems are subject to challenges and are not static. While the basics of any religion might change only slowly, the way a religion is expressed and practiced is constantly evolving. Almost all religions include subgroups and different schools. How do different cultural communities and religious faiths explain and respond to disability? Cultures and religious practices are ever-changing, and there may be many subgroups within each culture and religion, making it impossible to give definitive answers to specific questions.

People with disabilities of all faiths are more likely than people without disabilities to report that they have ever prayed for their own health. Among people with disabilities, 70.9 percent say they have prayed for their health, compared to only 48.4 percent of people without disabilities (National Health Interview Study, 2002). Women with disabilities aged 45 to 64 are most likely to pray for health (77.2%), while men without disabilities aged 18 to 44 years are the least likely to pray for health (37.7%). A poll by the National Organization on Disability (2003) of people faced with a disability found that a majority reported an increase in their religious faith. Many others, however, reported that coping with their disability had little or no effect on their spiritual life, while a few people said that coping with their disability led them to seek religious beliefs.

The works of many writers, sculptors, painters, and composers illustrate the role of religion in the social and historical context of disability. Intertwined throughout history are myriad religious influences on artistic representations. The Renaissance gave us classical artistic representations of faith-based hope for persons with disabilities, including New Testament depictions of miracles; the Reformation questioned divine goodness amid the pain and suffering existing in the world; and representations of disabilities across religions attempted to explain disability through the temperament of the gods. From biblical treatises on pain and suffering to records of cures and miracles of faith, religion has played a major role in attitudes toward disability throughout history.

A Mayan celebration includes a dance celebrating elders with disabilities in a respectful and understanding manner. Dancers enter the stage using canes as support and struggle to come together for the dance. The dance illustrates the loneliness and alienation of the aged who have a disability— laborious steps and slow, melancholy music. Once in a circle, the dancers take hold of the cane of the person in front of them and find support from each other as the music quickens and the dancers' steps become more light-hearted and spry.

For centuries, people with disabilities have served as cultural objects, rather than as active creators of culture and media. Generally, people with disabilities have not decided how they would be portrayed, nor have they participated in the creation of cultural products that dealt with disability. Instead, artists and authors have used various disabilities to convey ideas about evil, suffering, grace, and human nature.

One example is Rembrandt von Rijn's etching *Peter and John Healing the Cripple at the Gate of the Temple* from 1659. Another is Francisco de Goya's drawing *Beggars Who Get About on Their Own in Bordeaux* from 1824–1827. In both drawings, a man with a disability is the main character. Rembrandt's piece contains two other main characters as well—St. Peter and St. John, who stand over the "cripple" (the commonly accepted term of the time) in an attitude of both benevolence and authority. In this biblical story, faith and divine intervention bring about a cure of the man's disability.

Goya's drawing focuses more closely on the individual with a disability, a beggar riding in a crude but apparently workable wheelchair. The beggar appears dirty and disheveled, but also actively engaged in the world. Even the work's title emphasizes mobility and independence. Goya's beggar faces the viewer head on. He is portrayed as active, a person in motion, whereas Rembrandt's cripple sits passively, his back to the viewer, perhaps waiting to be healed so that he can then take part in the world around him.

Why are the two images so different? Is it because one is based on a religious theme, and the other focuses on contemporary nineteenth-century society? There is one more factor to consider: Francisco de Goya contracted a high fever in 1792 and lost his hearing. By the time he drew *Beggars Who Get About on Their Own in Bordeaux*, Goya had been deaf for 30 years.

DISABILITY AND EMPLOYMENT

In the United States, charity has had a major impact on public perceptions of people with disabilities since the nineteenth century. The rapid industrialization of the U.S. economy meant that people with physical impairments were often unemployed. Business owners accumulate profit through the efforts of workers; since people with disabilities were frequently viewed as less productive than others, employers usually passed them over. Therefore, disability often meant poverty. This fact could not really be blamed on the disabilities themselves; rather, it was because businesses and communities often failed to give opportunities to persons with disabilities.

Helen Keller, a woman who campaigned for social justice and whose life was later dramatized in a play and several movies called *The Miracle Worker*, emphasized this important distinction. Simply put, in a more inclusive society, people with disabilities would have equal opportunity to be employed. Yet few people understood this. Instead, they saw persons with disabilities as completely unable to work. Therefore, most persons with disabilities were denied jobs. Their families supported some, but others had no such support available. These individuals found themselves having to beg—just like the beggars that had roamed European streets for centuries.

Some people used media to aid their efforts to solicit money from strangers, with pleas that were something like: *Being unable to walk due to an injured spine, the only income I have is what I receive from you, my dear friends. Your smallest contribution will be highly appreciated. Thank you. I trust you will not regret it.*

Cards or signs like this one carried a quick, compelling message, urging the recipient to take pity on the individual with a disability and make a donation. Eventually, organizations took over the task of raising money on behalf of persons with disabilities. Private charities adopted and refined the notions related to more traditional (street) begging. As mass media, such as magazines and television, grew into a major influence on citizens' beliefs— and on their financial decisions—charity organizations learned to create and convey powerful messages about disability. These messages deliberately played upon viewers' sympathies, in order to persuade them to contribute money.

DISABILITY AND LANGUAGE

Society's misconceptions about persons with disabilities are constantly being reinforced by disabling terms like "cripple," "spastic," and "idiot." Of course there is nothing inherently wrong with these terms; it is simply that their meaning has been substantially devalued by societal perceptions of persons with disabilities. In short, they have been turned into terms of abuse. Their continued use contributes significantly to the negative self-image of many persons with disabilities and, at the same time, perpetuates discriminatory attitudes and practices among the general public.

Referring to persons with disabilities as "handicapped" evokes images that the whole of life is a competition, as in horse racing or golf, and implies that they will not do well. Use of phrases such as the impaired, the disabled, the handicapped, the blind, the deaf, the deaf and dumb, and the crippled tend to dehumanize and objectify people with disabilities and should be avoided. It is offensive to represent someone as his or her impairment.

TOWARD ACCURATE REPRESENTATIONS

When representing persons with disabilities in the media, it is important to remember that the general public has limited insight into the environmental and social barriers that may prevent them from living full and active lives. Living with disability means being confronted with environmental and social barriers daily; any representation of persons with disabilities that does not reflect this experience is inaccurate and contributes to the continuation of such barriers. There are a number of important points to keep in mind when creating representations of disability in any medium.

Avoid depicting individuals with disabilities as receivers of charity. Show people with disabilities interacting with all people as equals, giving as well as receiving. All too often, individuals with disabilities are represented solely as recipients of pity.

Avoid one-dimensional characterizations of persons with disabilities. Wherever appropriate, portray persons with disabilities as having individual and complex personalities with a full range of emotions and activities. In common with all human beings, individuals with disabilities experience a variety of emotions such as happiness, depression, anger, and so on, and play an assortment of roles including lover, parent, provider, and so forth. This variation should be accurately reflected in media representations of persons with disabilities.

Keep away from representing physical or intellectual characteristics of any kind as the sole determinants of personality. Be particularly cautious about implying a correlation between impairment and evil.

Refrain from presenting persons with disabilities as objects of curiosity. Individuals with disabilities should be presented as members of an average population or a cast of characters. People with disabilities are generally able to participate in all aspects of community life and should be represented in a wide variety of roles and situations.

An individual with a disability should not be ridiculed or made the butt of a joke for having a disability. In the real world, people with visual impairments do not drive cars, play darts, or bump into everything in their path, despite the mythmaking of some script writers, rather limited comedians, and unscrupulous mainstream advertisers.

Avoid the sensational in portrayals of people with disabilities. Be especially cautious of the stereotype of persons with disabilities as either the victims or the perpetrators of violence. Resist representing characters with disabilities as having extraordinary abilities or attributes. To do so is to suggest that an individual with a disability must overcompensate and become superhuman to be accepted by society.

Avoid the "stiff upper lip" and "tough love" storyline that implies a character with a disability need only have the will and the right attitude to succeed.

Refrain from showing people with disabilities as sexually abnormal, sexually dead, or sexually degenerate. Instead, show individuals with disabilities in normal relationships expressing the same emotional and sexual needs and desires as other people. When representing people with disabilities in media, ensure that they are representative of the sexual, racial, ethnic, gender, and age divisions in the disabled population as a whole.

Persons with disabilities are rarely shown as integral and productive members of the community—as students, as teachers, as part of the workforce, or as parents. The absence of such representations feeds the notion that people with disabilities are inferior human beings who should be segregated. Apart from the exploitations and misrepresentations mentioned throughout this section, persons with disabilities are conspicuous by their absence from mainstream popular culture.

The subject of disability has long fascinated authors, artists, and members of the public. Because disabling conditions are so widespread and can affect any family at any time, everyone has a stake in trying to comprehend what it means to live with a disability. People look to cultural products for information, understanding, and interpretation of the disability experience. Media representations may offer accurate information and truthful insights or, just as likely, they may put forth myths, distortions, or outright falsehoods. For persons with disabilities, concern regarding representations of disability is one aspect of working to ensure a place in society in the present and in the future.

IV

The Future of Disability in Society

11

Future Social Issues for Persons with Disabilities

The two final chapters examine future issues of disability in society. This chapter focuses on the future of disability in society and some of the major issues that appear to be shaping the contemporary social roles of persons with disabilities. These issues include the continuing struggle for integration and inclusion, the preservation and enforcement of civil rights, the incorporation of issues of disability into discussions of diversity, new medical developments that raise many concerns for persons with disabilities, and the increasing importance of access and accessibility to information and technology. Though these are not the only issues that will likely play a significant role in shaping the social future of persons with disabilities, the issues discussed at length here are among those that have the potential to most profoundly affect the lives of persons with disabilities in the future. Chapter 12 examines the evolution of a disability culture and its social impact. The issues discussed in this part demonstrate the continuing importance of concepts of inclusion, access, diversity, and civil rights in lives of persons with disabilities.

INCLUSION AND INTEGRATION

As has hopefully been demonstrated, persons with disabilities have made significant inroads into society over the past several decades. These advances have occurred in many different parts of the world. In spite of all of the progress that has been made, the ongoing integration and inclusion of persons with disabilities still has a long way to go in altering social perceptions and classifications. In many less developed nations, the battle for inclusion has not even truly begun. In nations where integration has started, outdated social classifications can still inhibit the extent of successful inclusion.

In the United States and other technologically advanced societies, issues related to disability are still sidelined in social and political discourse. "Disability is generally not felt to be central to questions of how a society is constituted and how it is governed, nor is disability very often raised in the context of now-popular discussions of the reinvigoration of civil society" (Goggin & Newell, 2003, p. 57). Much of this is due to the ways that persons with disabilities continue to be perceived and classified. The increased avenues of access and opportunities in a wide array of areas have heightened the participation and presence of persons with disabilities in society. Many members of society, however, have yet to accept inclusion or integration of persons with disabilities. In many social and political decisions, the lack of acceptance still holds sway.

A glaring example of this lack of acceptance is how children with mental illnesses are treated. Tens of thousands of youths with mental illnesses around the United States are housed in jails or juvenile detention centers every year as they await community mental health services because the number of available treatment options is insufficient (Cable News Network, 2004). In June 2004, youths with mental illnesses in 33 states were being held in detention centers and, on average, were being held for longer periods of time than children who were facing criminal charges (Cable News Network, 2004). The nationwide lack of proper facilities for children with mental illness is one of many examples of how the innovations from inclusion have yet to make a real difference.

Even in situations where inclusion has been given a great deal of emphasis, there can still be considerable resistance. In education, where the inclusion of students with disabilities has been a key part of IDEA for three decades, there is still considerable resistance and objection to the inclusion of students with disabilities. The inclusion of students with disabilities in general education classrooms has been attacked as being too costly (Allis, 1996; Gubernick & Conlin, 1997; Howard, 1994); as giving students with disabilities too many rights (Bunch, 1998; Rachelson, 1997; Ramsingh, 1995); as giving students with disabilities an unfair advantage over other students (Howard, 1994); and even as evidence of the breakdown of the moral foundation of society (Nelson, 1997). The inclusion of students with disabilities has also been attacked as being detrimental to other students and to the entire education process (Dupre, 1997; Howard, 1994). Although all of these claims about inclusion can be soundly refuted (Jaeger & Bowman, 2002), they demonstrate a deep-seated distrust of inclusion in many parts of society that has not been overcome by three decades of inclusion in public schools.

Nevertheless, education may provide the best example of the successes of inclusion. The integration of students with disabilities into general education classrooms presents a tremendously stark contrast to the way these students were previously treated in education. Before IDEA and the mandate of inclusion, most children with disabilities were not allowed to attend public schools, and those who were usually received a minimal or nonexistent education. Persons with disabilities who went to public school before the implementation of IDEA often have rather startling stories, like being left alone in a closet with a few textbooks each day or being tied to a chair with rope each morning so that they would not be "disruptive" to other students. The integration of students with disabilities in general education classrooms shows that inclusion can make a tremendous difference in their lives.

Finding ways to overcome social resistance to inclusion will be very important for persons with disabilities in the coming years. Inclusion is the pathway to being genuinely integrated into and accepted as a part of society. Persons with disabilities must continue to strive for inclusion into all facets of society, while also finding new ways to educate others about the importance of inclusion.

ACCESS IN THE INFORMATION SOCIETY

Virtually every battle for disability rights has been about access in some way or other. There have been struggles for access to physical structures, to public spaces, to education, to employment, to government, to services, to businesses, to travel, and to many other aspects of social life. Though it cannot be said that complete access to any of these areas has been accomplished, the evolution of technology and its growing importance in daily life has created a pressing new area for access concerns. Computers and related ICTs are becoming more important in virtually every aspect of life.

Persons with disabilities have often benefited significantly from technological advances. Advances in technology often lead to assistive devices that can make a meaningful difference in the daily lives of people with disabilities. Technological advances have helped persons with disabilities in education, employment, and many other areas and have helped to make persons with disabilities secure a greater presence in society, becoming "more familiar and less frightening" to other people (Mairs, 1996, p. 127). Advances in information and communication technologies have whetted the appetite for information of persons with disabilities, making them "information hungry" and even "starved for information" (Cunningham & Coombs, 1997, p. 131). Many recent advances related to computer technology, however, are leaving persons with disabilities behind in the progression toward increased access to information.

Technological developments do at times create problematic situations for persons with disabilities. A technological advance that benefits most of society while not allowing access for individuals with disabilities actually becomes a type of oppression (Goggin & Newell, 2003). By not providing access for persons with disabilities, a new technology establishes a new benefit for other people and a new method of exclusion of persons with disabilities. Currently, the continual development of the World Wide Web and related ICTs is generating a situation in which much of the online world is utterly inaccessible to persons with disabilities.

Many computer technologies, many Internet service providers, most government Web sites, and virtually all commercial Web sites are inaccessible in some way to persons with a range of disabilities. As more information and services are moved to the Web and as more content becomes available exclusively online, these disparities in access will continue to expand and have stronger impacts on persons with disabilities. As ICTs continue to play greater roles in everyday life, and as they become increasingly vital to education and employment, lack of access will have the potential to create electronic barriers that parallel the physical barriers that predate disability rights laws. These electronic barriers threaten to greatly reduce the social presence and inclusion of persons with disabilities.

Actually, it is surprising that accessibility is not more highly regarded or more commonly employed in the development and implementation of information and communication technologies. Technologies that are designed to be accessible usually are easier to use and beneficial for all users, as well as having larger potential markets than similar technologies that are not accessible (Mueller, 2003; Slatin & Rush, 2003). It will be essential for persons with disabilities to make developers, producers, and distributors of information and communication technologies aware of the unquestionable importance of accessibility for persons with disabilities. It is also important for studies of accessibility to focus more on the specific types of access available and how accessibility is being achieved (Jaeger, 2003b). This area of access is a pressing concern for persons with disabilities to ensure that they are a part of the information society that will become increasingly important as new technologies are continually developed and implemented.

MEDICAL CLASSIFICATIONS AND THE NEW EUGENICS

Recent developments in medicine and related scientific advances raise numerous questions for persons with disabilities. Despite the fact that medical developments have often resulted in significant benefits for them, persons with disabilities have always had a problematic relationship with the medical profession. It was, after all, the medical community and related scientific researchers that forwarded and developed the ideas of eugenics, as well as sterilization and lobotomy procedures. Virtually every medical issue affects persons with disabilities, as advances in medicine are often described as new tools for "fixing" disability (Wolbring, 2003).

Persons with disabilities have historically been denied the right to make decisions about their own medical care (Tomasevsci, 1999). Though most people with disabilities have a much greater voice in their own care now, certain scientific developments are actually threatening the existence of persons with disabilities. The formal position of many governments is now a duality of claiming to respect the rights of persons with disabilities while simultaneously funding research for screening programs that are intended to limit the births of children with disabilities (Reinders, 2000). Concurrently, the right-to-die debate raises many concerns for persons with disabilities. The stereotype that life with a disability is not worth living lies at the heart of many arguments for aborting fetuses with disabilities and for the use of euthanasia, which is politely referred to as "assisted suicide," on persons with disabilities (Fitzgerald, 1999). These stereotypes are exacerbated by the common fear of developing a disability (Fitzgerald, 1999).

The ethical dimensions of using genetic screening to classify fetuses as having a disability must be carefully considered (Switzer, 2003). Genetic screening allows parents and doctors to make eugenics-like decisions about the unborn. Many tests have been developed, and many more are being developed, that allow parents to know if their unborn child has one of many identifiable conditions. In many cases, the test results may encourage the parents to abort the fetus. "It implies that it may be better for the child not to be born at all rather than to be born with a disability" (Asch, Gostin, & Johnson, 2003, p. 326). If parents are willing to abort a fetus because it has a disability, it demonstrates a clear belief by parents that life with a disability is without value. Such practices call into question respect for persons with disabilities and claims of the value of diversity throughout society. Such practices also contain many echoes of the eugenics programs of the past.

The issues are, at least, matters of private concern in most societies. The government is not externally enforcing decisions on the parents about whether to abort the fetus, which is a marked difference from eugenics laws of the past. However, at least one nation does have mandatory abortion laws related to the genetic screening of fetuses. Since 1994, China has made prenatal checkups compulsory, and fetuses are screened for many conditions. Under Chinese law, it is the doctors, not the parents, who make the decision of whether the fetus should be aborted (Ridley, 1999). China also continues to perform sterilizations on persons born with certain types of disabilities (Bulmer, 2003).

The question of ending a young life that has been classified as having a disability has even been extended beyond birth. A professor at Princeton University's Center for Human Values has argued that parents of infants with disabilities should have the right to kill the child within a certain period of time after birth and try again to have a child without a disability (Switzer, 2003). This assertion is so horrifying that it is hard to believe that it has been made. Consider if a similar assertion had been made in reference to a different characteristic. One might imagine that a faculty member who advocated the right to infanticide of female children would face a firestorm of criticism by the public and in the national media. The positions of this faculty member have basically gone unnoticed by the public and media, however. Suggestions of infanticide are not that far removed from another dangerous issue, the right-to-die debate and the practice of euthanasia.

The right-to-die debate centers on whether people should have the legal right to medically assisted suicide if they have certain medical conditions. Much of the right-to-die debate has been directed at not only terminal illnesses but also nonfatal disabilities. In terms of disabilities, the argument is made that death may be preferable to living with a disability. This idea also is disturbingly similar to arguments employed by supporters of the first eugenics movement. Such assertions also open the door to giving doctors the right to decide to euthanize patients with disabilities against their wishes.

Eugenicists originally argued for euthanasia of persons with disabilities in order to benefit the people, their families, and society as a whole, blurring the distinctions between a patient's right to die and the decision of a physician to kill a patient (Longmore, 2003). In Nazi Germany, films were produced that hinged on such blurring to prepare the population for the subsequent euthanasia program, which resulted in hundreds of thousands of deaths of persons with disabilities (Longmore, 2003; Reilly, 1991). Amazingly, some current advocates of the right to die similarly blur the lines between voluntary and involuntary euthanasia, emphasizing the burden of persons with disabilities on their families and on society (Longmore, 2003). These current advocates accept the most glaring stereotypes about the life of a person with a disability, assuming that persons with disabilities are helpless, dependent, unhappy, burdensome, and unable to live a meaningful life (Longmore, 2003).

These two medical issues, the termination of fetuses with disabilities and the potential use of euthanasia/assisted suicide on persons with disabilities, could redefine the social position of persons with disabilities. Both of these notions are premised on the eradication of disability, and thereby persons with disabilities, through medical science. Raising the specter of a new eugenics movement, these issues indicate that persons with disabilities may have a very tenuous place in society. It also indicates that the social classifications of persons with disabilities may not yet have developed very far beyond the historical classifications of disability as a scourge on society that must be eliminated.

PRESERVING AND PROTECTING LEGAL RIGHTS

Once legal rights are established, these rights are not necessarily permanent and guaranteed. With the passage of Section 504 of the Rehabilitation Act, IDEA, and the ADA, a wide-ranging and fairly comprehensive set of civil rights was established for persons with disabilities. The enacting of the law is far from the end of the struggle, unfortunately. Many organizations with responsibilities under the law do not comply with the law, such as the many physical structures that have remained inaccessible. Further, the rights established by laws can be altered by court cases, and courts acting to limit the impact of the laws have dramatically affected disability rights laws.

Many efforts by persons with disabilities have been focused on getting laws implemented. The nationwide Rehabilitation Act protests in 1977 and many subsequent organized actions were intended to compel the implementation of requirements under the laws. In many cases, encouragement or public pressure have been sufficient to inspire compliance with the laws. In other cases, persons with disabilities have used the legal enforcement mechanisms in the laws to bring actions against parties that refuse to fulfill their obligations under the laws. Some of these cases have created significant results, but most of the cases filed by persons with disabilities under the disability rights laws have not been successful. For example, in the first ten years after the passage of the ADA, up to 96 percent of cases brought under the law by persons with disabilities were lost (Davis, 2002; Lee, 2003).

The lack of success for cases involving the enforcement of civil rights of persons with disabilities is cause for concern. The vast majority of Supreme Court decisions related to disability rights have limited the laws, continually whittling down the extent and scope of their protections. Supreme Court holdings have limited the obligations that the laws created for state governments, local governments, employers, and places of public accommodation. The Supreme Court has also acted to limit who can receive protection under the laws by repeatedly holding that if a correction exists for a disability, the person cannot be considered to have a disability, regardless of whether the correction is realistically available to the person or whether the person wants the correction. The Supreme Court decisions holding that a correctable disability is not really a disability opens the door for the possibility that persons with disabilities may be forced to be "fixed" by medical advances, whether they wish to or not (Wolbring, 2003). Lower courts have primarily followed the lead of the Supreme Court, tending to limit the scope and impact of disability rights laws in holdings by finding that laws do not apply to the case at hand, that the laws are too broad to enforce, or that the plaintiffs do not actually have a disability.

The curtailments of the scope and impact of the ADA and other disability rights laws have not caused significant reaction in the legislative or executive branches of the federal government. "The ADA is not dead, but it has been wounded by the courts and almost ignored by a Congress and president that have moved on to other causes, other issues" (Switzer, 2003, p. 229). The reasons for these curtailments are hard to discern. It may be that courts are still dominated by judges who do not understand or value the rights of persons with disabilities. Or it may be that judges have been persuaded by the various criticisms of disability rights laws. There remains a perception among many people that the "disabled lobby is waging warfare against every other citizen" (Howard, 1994, p. 148). Perhaps this sort of thinking holds sway among some members of the judiciary.

Another potential reason relates to the historical tendency of society to try to maintain control over persons with disabilities. "Society tends to seek to control disability, whether it be through statistics, welfare, medical advances, or mundane technologies" (Goggin & Newell, 2003, p. 31). The judiciary's limitations of civil rights laws for persons with disabilities may be the function of a social mechanism trying to assert and maintain control. Regardless of the reasons, attention must be focused on the continual constricting by the courts of the civil rights that persons with disabilities have fought so hard to win.

As a result of the erosion of the ADA, the law has not had as dramatic an impact as it should have had in the lives of persons with disabilities. Employment provides a perfect example. A number of studies have found that the employment opportunities and economic situations of persons with disabilities did not meaningfully improve in the 1990s, as the ADA was coming into effect (Batavia & Schriner, 2001; Bound & Waidmann, 2002; Kruse & Schur, 2003; Schur, 2003a, 2003b). Had the goals and intended impacts of the ADA been given greater protection in courts and had the federal government more actively pursued enforcement, the ADA may have made the significant changes in the professional lives of persons with disabilities that were expected when the law was originally passed.

A key approach to protecting and preserving civil rights for persons with disabilities would be research that demonstrated the true impacts of the laws on the education, employment, and social integration of persons with disabilities. Such research would need to track changes statistically to see how the laws really are changing the fortunes of persons with disabilities (Collingnon, 1997). There is also serious need for research to track changes in social perceptions and classifications paralleling changes in the law. These kinds of research could be very helpful in persuading the public and the judiciary of the actual benefit of these laws and the need to keep them intact. Such research might be used in actual court cases to bolster claims under the laws.

Persons with disabilities need to keep aware of legal developments related to the laws and work to raise public awareness of these developments. One scholar has suggested that Congress needs to amend the ADA so that the definition of disability is clear enough that the judiciary cannot change its meaning (Lee, 2003). Lobbying, organized activities, and protests may be necessary to try to get the legislative and executive branches to pay attention to the restrictions that the judiciary is placing on the civil rights of persons with disabilities. Persons with disabilities have struggled far too long to establish civil rights and legal guarantees of access and inclusion to not work to preserve and protect these rights now.

MAKING DIVERSITY MORE INCLUSIVE

In many ways, "the new aspirations of people with disabilities have gone unnoticed and misunderstood by mainstream America" (Shapiro, 1993, p. 4).

These aspirations include both being included in mainstream society and being accepted as a distinct group of people who deserve respect. In some ways, persons with disabilities may have been more successful at the former than at the latter. Individual people with disabilities may be more successful at participating in society than persons with disabilities, as a group, are at convincing the rest of society that they deserve to be respected as a viable subculture.

When surveyed about social exclusion of minorities, members of the general population do not believe that the social exclusion of persons with disabilities is comparable to the social exclusion of women, racial minorities, religious minorities, or people of certain national origins (Francis & Silvers, 2000). One manifestation of this can be found in job listings. Oftentimes when a job posting encourages applications from minority candidates, persons with disabilities are not included in the list of minority groups.

Persons with disabilities have also had difficulty being accepted as a distinct group by other minority populations. Members of other minorities are hesitant to recognize persons with disabilities as part of diversity in society or in academia. "Previously legitimized groups such as Latinos or African Americans have been reluctant to admit disability into the multicultural arena" (Davis, 2002, p. 36). Readings related to disability are usually kept out of the curricula for multicultural studies programs, and those who study other minorities primarily resist the legitimating of disability studies programs in universities (Davis, 2002).

Persons with disabilities also have not been recognized as a specific population in certain legal contexts. In most states, disability is not part of hate crime statutes, which create stiffer penalties for criminal acts inspired by prejudice against members of specific populations. In the states that recognize disability in hate crime statutes, it can fall into a category of lower penalty along with crimes related to sexual orientation (Davis, 2002). In spite of limited recognition of the potential of crimes being committed specifically against an individual having a disability, persons with disabilities are particularly susceptible to being victims of crime. For example, as many as 85 percent of women with disabilities become victims of domestic violence, which is several times the average for all women (Davis, 2002). Similarly, because the treatment of persons with disabilities is so inhumane in certain parts of the world, it has been suggested that people with disabilities from certain nations should be able to seek asylum in the United States (Kanter & Dadey, 2000).

Disability does seem to be a very natural part of diversity. There is great diversity among persons with disabilities. Each different kind of disability has its own challenges and successes. People with different kinds of disabilities develop different skills, perspectives, and forms of creativity in dealing with situations. This range of experiences, perspectives, and skills allows persons with disabilities as a group to be able to contribute a great deal to the diversity of society. Whether society wishes to acknowledge the diversity of persons with disabilities, however, appears to be a separate issue.

Despite these obstacles to being included by society as an integral part of the spectrum of diversity, significant progress has been made at making disability more accepted in society. Individuals with disabilities "continue to forge bridges in all directions: to the nondisabled world, to each other, to the self" (Gill, 2001). The final chapter focuses on disability as its own culture and on the inroads that disability culture is slowly making into the rest of society.

12

Disability Culture in
a Nondisabled Society

At a national education conference in 2003, a group of educators attempted to isolate all of the issues of diversity that face the professors and students in teacher education. They wrote their feelings into a poem that addressed issues of race, gender, language, literacy, experience, ethnicity, culture, community, economics, and politics. There was a person with a disability in the group, a person who constantly challenged the group to see diversity beyond race and ethnicity. Every educator agreed that disability should be included, but no one felt comfortable writing disability explicitly into the poem.

The aspects of culture that link together persons with disabilities embody the themes explored in this book. These cultural attributes have been shaped by the social and legal classifications of and the reactions to disability. However, the presence of cultural unities among persons with disabilities evidences that disability is a natural part of human diversity. Increases in society's understanding of the cultural elements of disability would likely improve classifications of and reactions to disability. Other members of society are not the only ones who would benefit from a better understanding of the cultural elements of disability. The cultural bonds between persons with disabilities can function as a powerful unifier in ongoing efforts to secure greater inclusion, access, and civil rights in society.

The roles of disability in society have a sizable impact on persons with disabilities as individuals and as a group. These impacts have similar effects on many people and serve to create bonds between persons with disabilities. Regardless of the nature of the disability, everyone with a disability has had some very similar experiences when dealing with the social classifications of, reactions to, and representations of disability. Different people may have divergent responses to these social factors, but they all still must respond to these circumstances. In a very real way, the social oppressions, marginalizations, and exclusions faced by persons with disabilities do create bonds between them.

As people with disabilities have struggled to establish rights in the past few decades, they have also come to see themselves in a more positive and more unified light. Many persons with disabilities lacked an orientation toward civil rights prior to the passage of the disability rights laws, due, in a large part, to the ways disability is represented in society (Shapiro, 1994). The cumulative effect of the negative representations of disability had a disempowering impact on persons with disabilities. The social movement that arose from the fight to implement Section 504 of the Rehabilitation Act and to pass the ADA resulted in a much more self-empowered and organized population of persons with disabilities. This empowerment and organization gives persons with disabilities a greater awareness of the factors that unify their experiences. It has also had the effect of creating awareness of a disability culture.

To someone who has not experienced life with a disability, it may seem inappropriate to speak of a disability culture, since many of the defining traits of a culture are absent from persons with disabilities as a group. Unlike many other cultures, disability is not, under most circumstances, passed from parent to child. If you have a disability, your parents, your siblings, or your children might not. On the other hand, a close relative may have a different disability than you do. Other cultural traits are generally passed from generation to generation. If you have Tourette's syndrome, however, it does not mean that your parents do, too.

Disability is also not a trait that is encultured into children as they grow up. If a child is born to parents of a certain religious faith, it is likely that the child will be raised as a member of that faith. The child will be raised to believe what the religion teaches and practice what the religion requires. A child born to a parent with a disability, however, is not likely to be raised as though the child has a disability if he or she does not. Having a parent with a disability will certainly make a child more attuned to persons with disabilities, but it will not cause a set of beliefs, practices, or characteristics to be passed along. Further, disability is not unified by events or holidays on the calendar. Most cultures have a history that the members celebrate. Individuals with disabilities, on the other hand, have not been well recorded in history, so they have little detailed knowledge of their own history. Even if they did, persons with disabilities have precious little to celebrate in history. It is possible that the date of the signing of the ADA (July 26, 1991) may be a holiday someday, but it certainly is not now.

Though some factors make disability unique as a culture, it still is similar to other cultures in certain ways. Individuals with disabilities, no matter what their disability is, have shared experiences of struggle, of facing discrimination, and of learning to live somewhat differently than what has been deemed to be normal. They have faced the same social classifications of, reactions to, and representations of disability. They have struggled against similar barriers to access. They have all lived with disability being their "master status," the trait by which they are identified above all else (Albrecht & Verbugge, 2000; Charmaz, 2000). The shared experiences of having a disability—any disability—create cultural bonds between individuals with disabilities. People with disabilities often find it easier to discuss their deep feelings about life with a disability when they are talking to other people with disabilities. That comes from the sense of shared experience and a sense of solidarity.

People with disabilities are also united by certain social goals. All persons with disabilities, as a result of the challenges that they face in society, are linked by the goals of being accepted and included by society and having equal access. For persons with disabilities, true equality "incorporates the premise that all human beings—in spite of their differences—are entitled to be considered and respected as equals and have the right to participate in the social and economic life of society" (Rioux, 1994, pp. 85-86). To work toward this equality, persons with disabilities have found ways to work together to promote social goals of inclusion. In the battle for civil rights, people with disabilities became unified by mutual threats, such as exclusion and restriction of access (McGuire, 1994). This group cohesion served as the basis of disability rights organizations and protests against the mutual threats. This group cohesion will certainly be important in working toward equal access to the information and communication technologies that dominate the present age of information.

People with disabilities have formed many political organizations devoted to promoting civil rights and increasing access for individuals with disabilities, from local organizations that fight for accessible buses and access to government offices to national organizations that lobby for legislation (Fleischer & Zames, 2001). Organizations that campaign for civil rights for individuals with disabilities began in earnest in the 1960s and became a national force through protests in the 1970s (Bowe, 1979; Zola, 1994). In other instances, people with disabilities have created organizations that promote their free expression. For example, organizations that promote artistic endeavors for people with disabilities attempt to provide a "means of self-expression and pride in identity" (Corbett, 1999, p. 171).

It is not entirely accurate, however, to think of persons with disabilities as a completely unified and cohesive group. People with different types of disabilities have different goals and issues with access, accommodations, self-empowerment, and self-sufficiency, which significantly limit the cohesion of people with disabilities (McGuire, 1994). A wheelchair user faces certain issues of access and inclusion that a person with a hearing impairment does not, and vice versa. Someone with Down syndrome will have very different access and inclusion issues, experiences, and goals of self-sufficiency than a wheelchair user or a person with a hearing impairment. These differences in the issues faced by persons with different types of disabilities also work against the disability rights movement having a central publicly identifiable figure like other civil rights movements (Fleischer & Zames, 2001). In spite of these differences, persons with disabilities face the same general types of experiences, though the specifics vary. This diversity of experiences actually strengthens the culture, as people with different disabilities have different personal experiences and abilities to contribute to society.

Facing the same types of general experiences may also help shape the attitudes of many people with disabilities. Having a disability shapes a person's psychological character, being influenced by external events (the way one is treated by other people) and internal events (how one thinks and feels about oneself, as in terms of a disability). One scholar has suggested that people with disabilities tend to share certain personality traits:

- Accepting the differences between people
- Accepting human vulnerability and recognizing the need to help others
- Handling uncertainty and unpredictability
- Finding the humor in disabilities and the problems they cause
- Managing multiple tasks simultaneously
- Being highly oriented toward future goals and possibilities
- Being attuned to closure in personal communication
- Being flexible, creative, and inspired in situations of limited resources or nontraditional modes of operation. (Gill, 1995)

Clearly, many of these traits are helpful in dealing with the unique everyday life experiences of a person with a disability. Though not every person with a disability will possess all of these characteristics, many people with disabilities have developed some or all of these traits as a means of surviving and thriving in society.

Most persons with disabilities are accustomed to being ready to deal with unexpected circumstances. Very surprising circumstances may occur when an assistive device unexpectedly ceases to be helpful. Such instances, however, can really inspire determination and resourcefulness. William, a graduate student, was most surprised one late afternoon when his wheelchair broke. An axle snapped when he hit a corner and a side of the chair collapsed as the chair tipped from the broken axle. He, of course, was knocked out of his chair in the accident. With no use of his legs at all, William only had the option of crawling. Making matters more interesting was the fact that he was on the third floor of a building on campus to drop off a paper in a professor's mailbox, and no one was around on that floor at the time who could lend him a hand.

William first crawled down the hallway to the elevator. Leaning his back against the wall, he reached up to hit the button for the elevator, only to discover that he was not quite able to reach the button. So, he then crawled back to the opposite end of the hallway to the stairs. He first tried yelling down to see if anyone would hear him. When that yielded no response, he then slowly lowered himself down the stairs. Sliding sideways and moving his legs one at a time down each stair, it took him fifteen minutes to reach the second floor, tearing his pants along the way.

Fortunately, the professor for whom William had left a paper was now heading upstairs to check his mailbox. He was more than a little surprised to find William sitting on the stairs. After William explained his situation, the professor got some assistance and they carried William down to the front office on the first floor and called one of his friends to bring his spare chair from his apartment nearby. While they were waiting for his friend to arrive, William mentioned to the professor that he did get the paper turned in before all this happened. The professor responded, "Well, you certainly are getting an A-plus for effort."

People with disabilities have even begun to develop their own slang terms for concepts unique to the experience of having a disability. "Crip" and "cripple" subvert traditional slurs used against persons with disabilities and turn them around in the same manner that other minority groups have turned the hate words of others into personal affirmatives. This meaning of "crip" has led to the affirmative slogan "Crip is hip," a sign of disability pride and affirmation that has adorned T-shirts, bumper stickers, and posters. An "inspiration station" refers to situations in which nondisabled people view a person with a disability as inspiring. This term relates to the odd tendency of many members of the general population to claim that an individual with a disability is an inspiration or a hero, even if that person with a disability is merely going about daily activities. "Disabled person" is now even used by some people with disabilities to identify an individual who takes pride in being a person with a disability. The use of these terms by persons with disabilities demonstrates a rejection of the social stigma of disability and an embrace of disability culture.

To some persons with disabilities, disability culture can be a source of support and pride. It can be seen as having a wide and diverse literature (Brown, 1995). People who embrace membership in disability culture also often work to challenge social classifications of persons with disabilities as being passive and dependent by asserting personal empowerment (Barnartt & Scotch, 2001). For persons with disabilities, pride in disability culture also embraces the experiential values that relate to disability, emphasizing the value of self-determination, personal connections, interdependence, and human community (Longmore, 2003). The communitarian and nurturing impulses of disability culture can be particularly important to individuals who acquire a disability as an adult. The cultural connections can help to erode feelings of isolation and loss of identity (Fleischer & Zames, 2001). Together, all these different cultural connections can create a greater social consciousness about persons with disabilities and bring further empowerment to persons with disabilities.

The unifying factors for individuals with disabilities reflect the growing presence of individuals with disabilities in society. Access, inclusion, diversity, and civil rights have given individuals with disabilities entrance to many elements of society that were previously closed. The implementation and expansion of access, inclusion, diversity, and civil rights have also allowed individuals with disabilities to begin recognizing the similarities in their own lives and experiences. As more individuals with disabilities work together, share their experiences, and research the implications of disability, persons with disabilities have begun to be able to better understand disability as a personal experience and as a collective experience.

FACING FORWARD, LOOKING AHEAD

The topics in this book resist any type of traditional conclusion. Everything discussed here is an ongoing process. Persons with disabilities are working for, and often gaining, access to and inclusion in society and the accompanying legal rights in much of the world. When rights are gained, they must be protected and extended to other parts of the world. Each right that is established lays the groundwork for the next right that has to be established. New social, legal, and technological developments will continually create issues of inclusion, access, diversity, and civil rights that persons with disabilities will have to address. There is no real end point to the social processes in which persons with disabilities live. A time may come one day when persons with disabilities have full social equality in every nation and culture around the world. Any such time is so far in the distant future, however, that it remains an almost unthinkable goal.

Yet there have been many victories, progresses, and successes in the past few decades in many countries that cannot be diminished. The social world that a person with a disability experiences today in the United States, Europe, Australia, and a number of other places is radically different than the social world of even thirty years ago. Each individual who experiences these social and legal changes reinforces the value and importance of these changes. Each person with a disability who is included in society also demonstrates to other people the great changes that have occurred and, maybe, reminds those other people of the humanity of persons with disabilities. Inclusion, access, and civil rights can promote awareness and understanding of persons with disabilities among all members of society.

The changes in society also can be seen in the growing comprehension of the historical experiences of persons with disabilities. In March 2003, California's governor issued an official apology for the state's eugenics activities.

This made California the fifth of the 32 U.S. states with eugenics laws to issue a formal apology; the other states are Virginia, North Carolina, Oregon, and South Carolina (Cable News Network, 2003). Wake Forest University has also officially apologized for the involvement of its medical school in North Carolina's sterilization program (Gomstyn, 2003). Hardly a torrent of recognition, but it is enough to show that some leaders are beginning to realize the social significance of acknowledging the ways that persons with disabilities have been mistreated in the past.

Hopefully, this book has successfully conveyed the importance of the many social roles of disability in shaping the current conditions that persons with disabilities experience in their daily lives. Despite the social and legal gains for persons with disabilities in the past few decades and the accompanying realization of greater empowerment for individuals with disabilities, there are still many social issues to be addressed and social barriers to be overcome. As we have tried to demonstrate, the range of social roles of disability is complex and multifaceted, affecting virtually every aspect of the lives of persons with disabilities. New issues such as technological and medical advances develop in ways that will continue to challenge persons with disabilities. Concepts of inclusion, access, diversity, and legal rights will continue to be extremely important to persons with disabilities as they continue to work to establish themselves as equal participants in every society.

As persons with disabilities face the future, they have much to work toward in continuing to improve their social position and much to celebrate in what has been already accomplished. In 1954, Albert Einstein admonished that even though the struggle for human rights would never be finished business, ceasing to continue that struggle would be the undoing of humankind (Einstein, 1994). People with disabilities should find solace and inspiration in this assertion. Though the fight for inclusion, access, diversity, and legal rights in society is unfinished and likely always will be so, there is tremendous pride in the huge social changes that persons with disabilities have caused. There is also an abundance of hope in how much has changed in so few years after thousands and thousands of years of no progress. Persons with disabilities are successfully making a genuine place for themselves as an accepted and equal part of society.

References

Abberly, P. (1987). The concept of oppression and the development of a social theory of disability. *Disability, Handicap and Society, 2*, 5–20.

Abram, S. (2003). The Americans with Disabilities Act in higher education: The plight of disabled faculty. *Journal of Law and Education, 32*, 1–20.

Access Now, Inc. v. Southwest Airlines Co., Case No. 02-21734-CIV-SEITZ/BANDSTRA U.S. D.C., S. D. FL. (Oct. 18, 2002).

Air Carrier Access Act, 49 U.S.C.A. § 41705 (1986).

Albertsons, Inc. v. Kirkingburg, 527 U.S. 555 (1999).

Albrecht, G. L. (1992). *The disability business: Rehabilitation in America*. Newbury Park, CA: Sage.

Albrecht, G. L., & Verbugge, L. M. (2000). The global emergence of disability. In G. L. Albrecht, R. Fitzpatrick, & S. C. Scrimshaw (Eds.), *The handbook of social studies in health and medicine* (pp. 293–307). London: Sage.

Albrecht, G. L., Walker, V. G., & Levy, J. A. (1982). Social distance from the stigmatized: A test of two theories. *Social Science and Medicine, 16*, 1319–1327.

Allis, S. (1996, November 4). The struggle to pay for special ed. *Time*, 82–83.

Alvarez v. District Director of U.S. Immigration and Naturalization Service, 539 F.2d 1220, 1224, *cert. denied* 430 U.S. 918 (1976).

Americans with Disabilities Act (ADA), 42 U.S.C.A. § 12101 *et seq.* (1990).

Americans with Disabilities Act (ADA) regulations, 28 C.F.R. § 35 *et seq.* & 29 C.F.R. 1630 *et seq.*

Architectural Barriers Act of 1968, 42 U.S.C.A. § 4151 *et seq.* (1968).

Arnold, J. B., & Dodge, H. W. (1994). Room for all. *American School Board Journal, 181*(10), 22–26.

Asch, A., Gostin, L. O., & Johnson, D. M. (2003). Respecting persons with disabilities and preventing disability: Is there a conflict? In S. S. Herr, L. O.

Gostin, & H. H. Koh (Eds.), *The human rights of persons with intellectual disabilities* (pp. 319–346). New York: Oxford University Press.

Aschmann, A. (2002). Providing intellectual access to cooperative extension materials. *Quarterly Bulletin of the International Association of Agricultural Information Specialists, 47*(3/4), 89–92.

Bacon, F. (1985). Of deformity. In J. Pitcher (Ed.), *The essays* (pp. 191–192). New York: Penguin Books.

Baker, B. (2002). The hunt for disability: The new eugenics and the normalization of school children. *Teachers College Record, 10*(4), 663–703.

Baldwin, M. (1997). Can the ADA achieve its employment goals? *Annals of the American Academy of Political and Social Science, 549,* 37–52.

Ball, M. (1990). *Professional wrestling as ritual drama in American popular culture.* New York: Edwin Mellen Press.

Ballard, J., Ramirez, B. A., & Weintraub, F. J. (Eds.). (1982). *Special education in America: Its legal and governmental foundations.* Reston, VA: Council for Exceptional Children.

Barnartt, S., & Scotch, R. (2001). *Disability protests: Contentious politics 1970–1999.* Washington, DC: Gallaudet University Press.

Barnes, C. (1990). *Cabbage syndrome: The social construction of dependence.* Lewes: Falmer.

Bartlett v. New York State Board of Law Examiners, 790 F. Supp. 1094 (S.D.N.Y. 1997).

Barton, L. (1996). Sociology and disability: Some emerging issues. In L. Barton (Ed.), *Disability and society: Emerging issues and insights* (pp. 3–17). London: Addison Wesley Longman.

Batavia, A. I., & Schriner, K. (2001). The Americans with Disabilities Act as engine of social change: Models of disability and the potential of a civil rights approach. *Policy Studies Journal, 29,* 690–702.

Bates, F. L., & Peacock, W. G. (1989). Conceptualizing social structure: The misuse of classification in structural modeling. *American Sociological Review, 54*(4), 565–577.

Battye, L. (1966). The Chatterley syndrome. In P. Hunt (Ed.), *Stigma: The experience of disability.* London: Geoffrey Chapman.

Baynton, D. C. (2001). Disability and the justification of inequality in American history. In P. K. Longmore & L. Umansky (Eds.), *The new disability history: American perspectives* (pp. 33–57). New York: New York University Press.

Bednarek, M. (1993, February). Intellectual access to pictorial information. *Australian Library Journal,* 33–46.

Berger, R. (2001). Immigration and mental health: Principles for successful social work practice. In R. Perez-Koenig & B. Rock (Eds.), *Social work in the ear of devolution* (pp. 159–176). New York: Fordham University Press.

Berube, M. (1997, May 30). The cultural representation of people with disabilities affects us all. *Chronicle of Higher Education,* B4–B5.

Bessis, S. (1995). *From social exclusion to social cohesion: A policy agenda.* Paris: UNESCO.

Bick, J. (2000). Americans with Disabilities Act and the Internet. *Albany Law Journal of Science and Technology, 10,* 205–227.

Biesold, H. (1999). *Crying hands: Eugenics and deaf people in Nazi Germany* (W. Sayers, Trans.). Washington, DC: Gallaudet University Press. (Original work published in 1988)

Biklen, D., & Bogdan, R. (1982). Media portrayals of disabled people: A study in stereotypes. *Interracial Books for Children Bulletin, 4*(6), 7.

Black, R. (2004). Feature films: Public perception of disability. In C. A. Bowman & P. T. Jaeger (Eds.), *A guide to high school success for students with disabilities* (pp. 36–44). Westport, CT: Greenwood.

Blakeman, J. (2000). The exclusion of mentally ill aliens who may pose a danger to others: Where does the real threat lie? *University of Miami Inter-American Law Review, 31,* 287–332.

Blanck, P. D., Hill, E., Siegal, C. D., & Waterstone, M. (2003). *Disability civil rights law and policy.* St. Paul, MN: Thomson/West.

Board of Trustees of the University of Alabama v. Garrett, 531 U.S. 356 (2001).

Bogdan, R. (1988). *Freak show: Presenting human oddities for amusement and profit.* Chicago: University of Chicago Press.

Boorstin, D. J. (1989). *Hidden history: Exploring our secret past.* New York: Vintage.

Booz Allen Hamilton. (2002). *International e-economy benchmarking: The world's most effective policies for the e-economy.* London: Author.

Bound, J., & Waidmann, T. (2002). Accounting for recent declines in employment rates among working-aged men and women with disabilities. *Journal of Human Resources, 37,* 231–250.

Boutilier v. Immigration and Naturalization Service, 363 F.2d 927 (N.Y.), *affirmed* 387 U.S. 118 (1966).

Bowe, F. (1979). Handicapping America: Barriers to disabled people. In J. P. Hourihan (Ed.), *Disability: Our challenge* (pp. 87–106). New York: Teachers College Press.

Bowe, F. G. (1993). Access to the information age: Fundamental decisions in telecommunications policy. *Policy Studies Journal, 21*(4), 765–774.

Bowker, G. C., & Star, S. L. (1999). *Sorting things out: Classification and its consequences.* Cambridge, MA: MIT Press.

Bowman, C. A., & Jaeger, P. T. (2003, April). *Making diversity more inclusive: Toward a theory for the representation of disability.* Paper presented at the 2003 American Education Research Association Conference, Chicago, IL.

Bowman, C. A., & Jaeger, P. T. (2004). Disability in literature. In C. A. Bowman & P. T. Jaeger (Eds.), *A guide to high school success for students with disabilities* (pp. 44–56). Westport, CT: Greenwood.

Boyer, C. (2000). Libraries and Section 508 of the Rehabilitation Act. *Library Hi Tech News, 17*(5), 27–29.

Braddock, D. L., & Parish, S. L. (2001). An institutional history of disability. In G. L. Albrecht, K. D. Seelman, & M. Bury (Eds.), *Handbook of disability studies* (pp. 11–68). Thousand Oaks, CA: Sage.

Bragg, L. (1997). From the mute god to the lesser god: Disability in medieval Celtic and Old Norse literature. *Disability and Society, 12,* 165–177.

Brandt, E., & Pope, A. (1997). *Enabling America: Assessing disability and rehabilitation in America.* Washington, DC: National Academy Press.

Branson, J., & Miller, D. (2002). *Damned for their difference: The cultural construction of deaf people as disabled.* Washington, DC: Gallaudet University Press.

Breckenridge, C. A., & Vogler, C. (2001). The critical limits of embodiment: Disability's criticism. *Public Culture, 13*(3), 349–357.

Brown v. Board of Education, 347 U.S. 483 (1954).

Brown, S. (1995). A celebration of diversity: An introductory, annotated bibliography about disability culture. *Disability Studies Quarterly, 15*(4), 36–56.

Brown, T. J. (1998). *Dorothea Dix: New England reformer.* Cambridge, MA: Harvard University Press.

Bryan, W. V. (1996). *In search of freedom: How persons with disabilities have been disenfranchised from the mainstream of American society.* Springfield, IL: Charles C. Thomas.

Buck v. Bell, 274 U.S. 200 (1927).

Bulmer, M. (2003). *Francis Galton: Pioneer in heredity and biometry.* Baltimore: Johns Hopkins University Press.

Bunch, E. A. (1998). School discipline under the Individuals with Disabilities Education Act: How the stay-put provision limits schools in providing a safe learning environment. *Journal of Law and Education, 27*, 315–321.

Burgdorf, M., & Burgdorf, R. L. (1976). History of unequal treatment: The qualifications of handicapped persons as a "suspect class" under the equal protection clause. *Santa Clara Law Review, 15*, 855–910.

Burgdorf, R. L. (Ed.). (1980). *The legal rights of handicapped persons.* Baltimore: Paul H. Brookes.

Burgdorf, R. L. (1997). "Substantially limited" protection from disability discrimination: The special treatment model and misconstructions of the definition of disability. *Villanova Law Review, 42*, 409–585.

Cable News Network. (2003, March 13). *California apologizes for sterilization law.* Available: http://www.cnn.com.

Cable News Network. (2004, July 7). *Report: Jails warehouse mentally ill kids.* Available: http://www.cnn.com.

Carlson, S. (2004). Left out online: Electronic media should be a boon for people with disabilities, but few colleges embrace the many new technologies that could help. *Chronicle of Higher Education, 50*(40), A23.

Cary, K., & Ogburn, J. L. (2000). Developing a consortial approach to cataloging and intellectual access. *Library Collections, Acquisitions, and Technical Services, 24*, 45–51.

Charlton, J. I. (1998). *Nothing about us without us: Disability oppression and empowerment.* Berkeley: University of California Press.

Charmaz, K. (2000). Experiencing chronic illness. In G. L. Albrecht, R. Fitzpatrick, & S. C. Scrimshaw (Eds.), *The handbook of social studies in health and medicine* (pp. 277–292). London: Sage.

Chen, H., & Rasmussen, E. M. (1999). Intellectual access to images. *Library Trends, 48*(2), 291–302.

Chen, S. (1990). European and Asian immigration into the United States in comparative perspective, 1820s to 1920s. In V. Yans-McLaughlin (Ed.), *Immigration reconsidered: History, sociology, and politics* (pp. 37–75). New York: Oxford University Press.

Cherry v. Matthews, 419 F. Supp. 922 (D.D.C. 1976).

Christensen, C. (1996). Disabled, handicapped or disordered: "What's in a name?" In C. Christensen & F. Rizvi (Eds.), *Disability and the dilemmas of education and justice* (pp. 63–78). Buckingham: Open University Press.

Church, R. L., & Marston, J. R. (2003). Measuring accessibility for people with a disability. *Geographical Analysis, 35*(1), 83–96.

Cirillo, S. E., & Danford, R. E. (Eds.). (1996). *Library buildings, equipment, and the ADA: Compliance issues and solutions.* Chicago: American Library Association.

City of Cleburne v. City of Cleburne Living Center, Inc., 473 U.S. 432 (1985).

Civil Rights Act, 42 U.S.C.A. sec. 1971 *et seq.* (1964).

Cohen, D. A. (1993). Private lives in public spaces: Marie Stopes, the mothers' clinic and the practice of contraception. *History Workshop, 35,* 95–116.

Colker, R. (1999). The Americans with Disabilities Act: A windfall for defendants. *Harvard Civil Rights-Civil Liberties Law Review, 34,* 99–162.

Colker, R., & Tucker, B. P. (1998). *The law of disability discrimination* (2nd ed.). Cincinnati: Anderson.

Collingnon, F. C. (1997). Is the ADA successful? Indicators for tracking gains. *Annals of the American Academy of Political and Social Science, 549,* 129–147.

Comaromi, J. P. (1990). Summation of classification as an enhancement of intellectual access to information in an online environment. *Cataloging and Classification Quarterly, 11*(1), 99–102.

Connolly v. General Construction Co., 269 U.S. 385 (1926).

Corbett, J. (1999). Disability arts: Developing survival strategies. In P. Reitsh & S. Reiter (Eds.), *Adults with disabilities: International perspectives in the community* (pp. 171–181). Mahwah, NJ: Lawrence Erlbaum.

Corker, M., & French, S. (Eds.). (1999). *Disability discourse.* Buckingham: Open University Press.

Covey, H. C. (1998). *Social perceptions of people with disabilities in history.* Springfield, IL: Charles C. Thomas.

Cowan, R. S. (1985). *Sir Francis Galton and the study of heredity in the nineteenth century.* New York: Garland.

Craig v. Boren, 429 U.S. 190 (1976).

Cunningham, C., & Coombs, N. (1997). *Information access and adaptive technology.* Phoenix, AZ: Oryx Press.

Dahl, R. A. (1998). *On democracy.* New Haven, CT: Yale University Press.

Dahl, R. A. (2001). *How democratic is the American Constitution?* New Haven, CT: Yale University Press.

Daley v. Koch, 639 F. Supp. 289 (D.D.C. 1986).

D'Amico v. New York State Board of Bar Examiners, 813 F. Supp. 217 (W.D.N.Y. 1993).

Daniels, M. (1997). *Benedictine roots in the development of deaf education: Listening with the heart.* Westport, CT: Bergin and Garvey.

Darian v. University of Massachusetts Boston, 980 F. Supp. 77 (D.Mass. 1987).

Daunt, P. (1991). *Meeting disability: A European response.* London: Cassell Education.

Davis, L. J. (1997). Constructing normalcy: The bell curve, the novel, and the invention of the disabled body in the nineteenth century. In L. J. Davis (Ed.), *The disability studies reader* (pp. 9–29). New York: Routledge.

Davis, L. (1999). Riding with the man on the escalator: Citizenship and disability. In M. Jones & L. A. B. Marks (Eds.), *Disability, divers-ability, and legal change* (pp. 65–74). Boston: Martinus Nijhoff.

Davis, L. J. (2000). Dr. Johnson, Amelia, and the discourse of disability in the eighteenth century. In H. Duetsch & F. Nussbaum (Ed.), *Defects: Engendering the modern body* (pp. 54–74). Ann Arbor: University of Michigan Press.

Davis, L. J. (2002). *Bending over backwards: Disability, dismodernism and other difficulty positions.* New York: New York University Press.

De Hamel, C. (1994). *A history of illuminated manuscripts* (2nd ed.). New York: Phaidon Press.

Deines-Jones, C. (1996). Access to library Internet services for patrons with disabilities: Pragmatic considerations for developers. *Library Hi Tech, 14*(1), 57–64.

DeLaet, D. L. (2000). *U.S. immigration policy in an age of rights.* Westport, CT: Praeger.

Demleitner, N. W. (1997). The fallacy of social citizenship, or the threat of exclusion. *Georgetown Immigration Law Journal, 12,* 35-64.

Department of Commerce. (2000). *Falling through the Net: Toward digital inclusion.* Available: http://search.ntia.doc.gov/pdf/fttn00.pdf.

Department of Commerce. (2002). *A nation online: How Americans are expanding their use of the Internet.* Available: http://www.ntia.doc.gov/ntiahome/dn/index.html.

Department of Justice. (2001). *Information technology and people with disabilities: The current state of federal accessibility.* Available: http://www.usdoj.gov/crt/508/report/content.htm.

Dilevko, J., & Dali, K. (2003). Electronic databases for readers' advisory services and intellectual access to translated fiction not originally written in English. *Library Resources and Technical Services, 47*(3), 80–95.

Disability Rights Commission (United Kingdom). (2004). *The Web: Access and inclusion for disabled people.* London: Stationery Office.

Dispenza, M. L. (2002). Overcoming the new digital divide: Technology accommodations and the undue hardship defense under the Americans with Disabilities Act. *Syracuse Law Review, 52,* 159–181.

Doyle, B. (1996). *Disability discrimination: The new law.* Bristol, UK: Jordans.

Doyle, B. (1997). Enabling legislation or dissembling law? The Disability Discrimination Act 1995. *Modern Law Review, 60*(1), 64–78.

Drimmer, J. C. (1993). Cripples, overcomers, and civil rights: Tracing the evolution of federal legislation and social policy for people with disabilities. *UCLA Law Review, 40,* 1341–1410.

Dunn v. I.N.S., 499 F.2d 856 (9th Cir. 1974).

Dupre, A. P. (1997). Disability and public schools: The case against "inclusion." *Washington Law Review, 72,* 775–858.

Durant, W. (1944). *Caesar and Christ.* New York: Simon and Schuster.

Dyer, R. (1988). *Heavenly bodies: Film stars and society.* London: St. Martin's Press.

Edwards, M. L. (1997). Deaf and dumb in ancient Greece. In L. Davis (Ed.), *The disability studies reader* (pp. 29–51). New York: Routledge.

E. E. Black Limited v. Marshall, 497 F. Supp. 1088 (1980).

E-government Act of 2002, P.L. 107–347 (2002).

Einstein, A. (1994). *Ideas and opinions* (A. Lichtman, Ed.). New York: Modern Library.

Eisenberg, M. G. (1982). Disability as stigma. In M. G. Eisenberg, C. Griggins, & R. J. Duval (Eds.), *Disabled people as second-class citizens* (pp. 3–12). New York: Springer.

Ellison, J. (2004). Accessing the accessibility of fifty United States government Web pages: Using Bobby to check on Uncle Sam. *First Monday, 9*(7). Available: http://www.firstmonday.org/issues/issue9_7/ellison/index.html.

Ennes, A., & Smit, C. R. (2001). *Screening disability: Essays on cinema and disability.* Lanham, MD: University Press of America.

European Union. (1996). *Resolution of the council and the representatives of the governments of the member states of inequality of opportunity for people with disabilities.* Official Journal 13.01.1997. Brussels: Author.

European Union. (2001). *E-inclusion: The information society's potential for social inclusion in Europe.* Available: http://europa.eu.int/comm/employment_social/soc-dial/info_soc/esdis/eincl_en.pdf.

Ex parte Fragoso, 11 F.2d 988 (D.C.Cal. 1926).

Ex parte Hosaye Sakaguchi, 277 F. 913 (9th Cir. 1922).

Ex parte Lee Sher Wing, 164 F. 506 (N.D. Cal. 1908).

Ex parte Li Dick, 174 F. 674 (D.C.N.Y. 1909).

Ex parte Wong Nung, 30 F.2d 766 (Cal. 1929).

Fagan, J. C., & Fagan, B. (2004). An accessibility study of state legislative websites. *Government Information Quarterly, 21,* 65–85.

Fair Housing Act of 1988, 42 U.S.C.A. § 1885 *et seq.* (1988).

Faustino v. Immigration and Naturalization Service, 302 F.Supp. 212 (S.D. N.Y. 1969).

Fay, G. O. (1899). Hartford and the education of the deaf. *American Annals of the Deaf, 44,* 419.

Feldblum, C. (2000). Definition of disability under federal anti-discrimination law: What happened? why? and what can we do about it? *Berkeley Journal of Employment and Labor Law, 21,* 91–165.

Ferrante, J. (1988). Biomedical versus cultural constructions of abnormality: The case of idiopathic hirsutism in the United States. *Culture, Medicine and Psychiatry, 12*(2), 219–238.

Fetzer, J. S. (2000). *Public attitudes toward immigration in the United States, France, and Germany.* Cambridge: Cambridge University Press.

Fine, M., & Asch, A. (1988). Disability beyond stigma: Social interaction, discrimination, and activism. *Journal of Social Issues, 44*(1), 3–21.

Finkelstein, V. (1980). *Attitudes and disabled people.* New York: World Rehabilitation Fund.

First, P. F., & Hart, Y. Y. (2002). Access to cyberspace: The new issue in educational justice. *Journal of Law and Education, 31,* 385–411.

Fitzgerald, J. (1999). Bioethics, disability and death: Uncovering cultural bias in the euthanasia debate. In M. Jones & L. A. B. Marks (Eds.), *Disability, diversability, and legal change* (pp. 267–282). Boston: Martinus Nijhoff.

Fleischer, D. Z., & Zames, F. (2001). *The disability rights movement: From charity to confrontation.* Philadelphia: Temple University Press.

146   REFERENCES

Foucault, M. (1965). *Madness and civilization: A history of insanity in the age of reason* (Richard Howard, Trans.). New York: Vintage.

Francis, L. P., & Silvers, A. (Eds.). (2000). *Americans with disabilities: Exploring implications of the law for individuals with disabilities.* New York: Routledge.

Frank, G. (1988). Beyond stigma: Visibility and self-empowerment of persons with congenital limb deficiencies. *Journal of Social Issues, 44,* 95–115.

French, R. S. (1932). *From Homer to Helen Keller: A social and educational study of the blind.* New York: American Foundation for the Blind.

Frey, W. (1984). Functional assessment in the '80s: A conceptual enigma, a technical challenge. In A. S. Halporn & M. J. Fuhrer (Eds.), *Functional assessment in rehabilitation* (pp. 11–43). Baltimore: Paul H. Brookes.

Friedlander, H. (1995). *The origins of Nazi genocide: From euthanasia to the final solution.* Chapel Hill: University of North Carolina Press.

Friedlander, H. (1999). Introduction. In H. Biesold, *Crying hands: Eugenics and deaf people in Nazi Germany* (pp. 1–12). Washington, DC: Gallaudet University Press.

Friedlander, H. (2002). Holocaust studies and the deaf community. In D. F. Ryan & J. S. Schuchman (Eds.), *Deaf people in Hitler's Europe* (pp. 15–31). Washington, DC: Gallaudet University Press.

Funk, R. (1987). Disability rights: From caste to class in the context of civil rights. In A. Gartner & T. Joe (Eds.), *Images of the disabled, disabling images* (pp. 7–30). New York: Praeger.

Galloway v. Superior Court of District of Columbia, 816 F. Supp. 12 (D.D.C. 1993).

Galton, F. (1883). *Inquiry into human faculty and its developments.* London: Macmillan.

Galton, F. (1889). *Natural inheritance.* London: Macmillan.

Galton, F. (1978). *Hereditary genius: An inquiry into its laws and consequences.* New York: St. Martin's Press. (Original work published 1869)

Garland, R. (1995). *The eye of the beholder: Deformity and disability in the Graeco-Roman world.* Ithaca, NY: Cornell University Press.

Garton, S. (2000). Writing eugenics: A history of classification practices. In M. Crotty, J. Germov, & G. Rodwell (Eds.), *"A race for a place": Eugenics, Darwinism, and social thought and practice in Australia* (pp. 9–18). Newcastle, AU: University of Newcastle Press.

Gaw, A. (1906). The development of the legal status of the deaf. *American Annals of the Deaf, 51,* 269–275, 401–423.

Gaw, A. (1907). The development of the legal status of the deaf. *American Annals of the Deaf, 52,* 1–12, 167–83, 229–245.

Gegiow v. Uhl, 239 U.S. 3 (1915).

Ghai, A. (2001). Marginalisation and disability: Experiences from the third world. In M. Priestley (Ed.), *Disability and the life course: Global perspectives* (pp. 26–37). Cambridge: Cambridge University Press.

Gibson, K. (2001). Better accessibility draws multiple markets. *Marketing News, 35*(2), 8.

Gill, C. J. (1995). A psychological view of disability culture. *Disabilities Studies Quarterly, 15*(4), 16–19.

Gill, C. J. (2001). Divided understandings: The social experience of disability. In G. L. Albrecht, K. D. Seelman, & M. Bury (Eds.), *Handbook of disability studies* (pp. 351–372). Thousand Oaks, CA: Sage.

Gillham, N. W. (2001). *A life of Sir Francis Galton: From African exploration to the birth of eugenics*. Oxford: Oxford University Press.

Gilliland, A. J. (1988). Introduction: Automating intellectual access to archives. *Library Trends, 38*, 495–499.

Gleeson, B. (1999). *Geographies of disability*. London: Routledge.

Goering, S. (2002). Beyond the medical model?: Disability, formal justice, and the exception for the "profoundly impaired." *Kennedy Institute of Ethics Journal, 12*(4), 373–388.

Goffman, E. (1963). *Stigma: Notes on the management of spoiled identity*. Englewood Cliffs, NJ: Prentice Hall.

Goggin, G., & Newell, C. (2000). An end to disabling policies? Toward enlightened universal service. *Information Society, 16*, 127–133.

Goggin, G., & Newell, C. (2003). *Digital disability: The social construction of disability in new media*. Lanham, MD: Rowman and Littlefield.

Gomstyn, A. (2003). Wake Forest Medical School apologizes for furthering state's sterilization campaign. *Chronicle of Higher Education*. Available: http://chronicle.com.

Gooding, C. (1996). *Blackstone's guide to the Disability Discrimination Act of 1995*. London: Blackstone.

Gould, S. J. (1996). *The mismeasure of man* (rev. ed.). New York Norton.

Graham v. Richardson, 403 U.S. 365 (1971).

Grand, S. A., Bernier, J. E., & Strohmer, D. C. (1982). Attitudes toward disabled persons as a function of social context and specific disability. *Rehabilitation Psychology, 27*, 165–174.

Gray, P. (1999). Cursed by eugenics. *Time, 153*(1), 84–85.

Grealy, L. (2003). *Autobiography of a face*. New York: Harper Collins.

Gritzer, G., & Arluke, A. (1985). *The making of rehabilitation: A political economy of medical specialization*. Berkeley, CA: University of California Press.

Gubernick, L., & Conlin, M. (1997, February 10). The special education scandal. *Forbes Magazine*, 66–70.

Guckenberger v. Boston University, 957 F. Supp. 306 (D.C. Mass. 1997); 974 F. Supp. 106 (D.C. Mass. 1997).

Guenther, K. (2002). Section 508 and your Web site. *Online, 26*(2), 71–75.

Hahn, H. (1983, March-April). Paternalism and public policy. *Society*, 36–46.

Hahn, H. (1988). The politics of physical difference: Disability and discrimination. *Journal of Social Issues, 44*(1), 39–47.

Hahn, H. (1997). New trends in disability studies: Implications for educational policy. In D. K. Lipsky & A. Gartner (Eds.), *Inclusion and school reform: Transforming America's classrooms* (pp. 315–328). Baltimore: Paul H. Brooks.

Hallenbeck, B. A., & Kauffman, J. M. (1994). Integrated special education: United States. In K. Mazurek & M. A. Winzer (Eds.), *Comparative studies in special education* (pp. 403–419). Washington, DC: Gallaudet University Press.

Hammond, A. S. (2002). Equality in the information age: The digital divide in the new millennium. *Cardozo Arts and Entertainment Law Journal, 20*, 135–156.

Handel, R. C. (1975). The role of the advocate in securing the handicapped child's right to an effective minimal education. *Ohio State Law Journal, 36*, 349–378.

Hansen, A. (1916). The education of the deaf in the Scandinavian countries. *Volta Review, 18*, 407.

Harasymiw, S. J., Horne, M. D., & Lewis, S. C. (1976). Disability social distance hierarchy for population subgroups. *Scandinavian Journal of Rehabilitation Medicine, 8*, 33–36.

Hawthorne, S., Denge, J., & Coombs, N. (1997). The law and library access for patrons with disabilities. *Information Technology and Disabilities, 3*(1). Available: http://www.rit.edu/~easi/itd/itdv04n1/article5.html.

Heberer, P. (2002). Targeting the "unfit" and radical public health strategies in Nazi Germany. In D. F. Ryan & J. S. Schuchman (Eds.), *Deaf people in Hitler's Europe* (pp. 49–70). Washington, DC: Gallaudet University Press.

Hernon, P., Reylea, H. C., Dugan, R. E., & Cheverie, J. F. (2002). *United States government information: Policies and sources.* Westport, CT: Libraries Unlimited.

Hervey, D. (1992). *The creatures that time forgot: Photography and disability imagery.* New York: Routledge.

Heumann, J. E. (1979). Handicap and disability. In J. P. Hourihan (Ed.), *Disability: Our challenge* (pp. 7–32). New York: Teachers College Press.

Hewett, F. (1974). *Education of exceptional learners.* Boston: Allyn and Bacon.

Hibbert, C. (1975). *The house of Medici.* New York: William Morrow.

Higgins, P. C. (1992). *Making disability: Exploring the social transformation of human variation.* Springfield, IL: Charles C. Thomas.

Hignite, K. B. (2000). The accessible association. *Association Management, 52*(13), 36–43.

Hill, K. D. (1986). Legal conflicts in special education: How competing paradigms in the Education for All Handicapped Children Act create litigation. *University of Detroit Law Review, 64*, 129–170.

Hobbs, T. & Westling, D. L. (1998). Inclusion, inclusion, inclusion: Promoting successful inclusion. *Teaching Exceptional Children, 31*, 12–19.

Horne, M. D. (1985). *Attitudes toward handicapped students: Professional, peer and parent reactions.* Hillsdale, NJ: Erlbaum.

Horne, M. D., & Ricciardo, J. L. (1988). Hierarchy of response to handicaps. *Psychological Reports, 62*, 83–86.

Horrigan, J. B., & Rainie, L. (2002). *Counting on the Internet.* Washington, DC: Pew Internet and American Life Project.

Howard, P. K. (1994). *The death of common sense: How law is suffocating America.* New York: Warner.

Huber, J. T., & Gillaspy, M. L. (1998). Social constructs and disease: Implications for a controlled vocabulary for HIV/AIDS. *Library Trends, 47*(2), 190–208.

Huefner, D. S. (1998). The Individuals with Disabilities Education Act amendments of 1997. *Education Law Reporter, 122*, 1103–1122.

Hunt, P. (1966). *Stigma: The experience of disability.* London: Geoffrey Chapman.

Imrie, R. (1996). *Disability and the city: International perspectives.* New York: St. Martin's.

Individuals with Disabilities Education Act (IDEA), 20 U.S.C.A. § 1400 *et seq.* (1975).

Individuals with Disabilities Education Act (IDEA) regulations, 34 C.F.R. § 300 *et seq.*

In re Di Simone, 108 F. 942 (E.D.La. 1901).

In re Hollinger, 211 F. Supp. 203 (E.D.Mich. 1962).

Intner, S. S. (1991). Intellectual access to patron-use software. *Library Trends, 40*(1), 42–62.

Jacko, J. A., & Hanson, V. L. (2002). Universal access and inclusion in design. *Universal Access in the Information Society, 2*, 1–2.

Jaeger, P. T. (2002). Section 508 goes to the library: Complying with federal legal standards to produce accessible electronic and information technology in libraries. *Information Technology and Disabilities 8*(2). Available: http://www.rit.edu/~easi/itd/itdv08n2/jaeger.html.

Jaeger, P. T. (2003a). The endless wire: E-government as global phenomenon. *Government Information Quarterly, 20*(4), 323–331.

Jaeger, P. T. (2003b). The importance of measuring the accessibility of the federal e-government: What studies are missing and how these issues can be addressed. *Information Technology and Disabilities, 9*(1). Available: http://www.rit.edu/~easi/itd/itdv09n1/jaeger.htm.

Jaeger, P. T. (2004a). Beyond Section 508: The spectrum of legal requirements for accessible e-government websites in the United States. *Journal of Government Information, 30*(4), 518–533.

Jaeger, P. T. (2004b). The social impact of an accessible e-democracy: The importance of disability rights laws in the development of the federal e-government. *Journal of Disability Policy Studies, 15*(1), 19–26.

Jaeger, P. T., & Bowman, C. A. (2002). *Disability matters: Legal and pedagogical issues of disability in education.* Westport, CT: Praeger.

Jaeger, P. T., & Thompson, K. M. (2003). E-government around the world: Lessons, challenges, and new directions. *Government Information Quarterly, 20*(4), 389–394.

Jaeger, P. T., & Thompson, K. M. (2004). Social information behavior and the democratic process: Information poverty, normative behavior, and electronic government in the United States. *Library and Information Science Research, 26*(1), 94–107.

Jenkins, R. (1991). Disability and social stratification. *British Journal of Sociology, 42*(4), 557–580.

Johnson, A. D. (2004). Assistive technology changes lives: Opening a window to the world. *Diversity Inc, 3*(3), 23–32.

Johnson, K. R. (2004). *The "huddled masses" myth: Immigration and civil rights.* Philadelphia: Temple University Press.

Jones, M., & Marks, L. A. B. (Eds.). (1999). *Disability, divers-ability, and legal change.* Boston: Martinus Nijhoff.

Jones, R. L. (1974). The hierarchical structure of attitudes toward the exceptional. *Exceptional Children, 40*(6), 430–436.

Kanayama, T. (2003). Leaving it all up to industry: People with disabilities and the Telecommunications Act of 1996. *Information Society, 19*, 185–194.

Kanner, L. (1964). *A history of the care and study of the mentally retarded.* Springfield, IL: Charles C. Thomas.

Kanter, A., & Dadey, K. (2000). The right to asylum for people with disabilities. *Temple Law Review, 73*, 1117–1158.

Keates, S., & Clarkson, P. J. (2003). Countering design exclusion: Bridging the gap between usability and accessibility. *Universal Access in the Information Society, 2,* 215–225.

Kennard, W. E., & Lyle, E. E. (2001). With freedom comes responsibility: Ensuring that the next generation of technologies is accessible, usable, and affordable. *CommLaw Conspectus, 10,* 5–22.

Kennedy, F. (1942). The problem of social control of the congenitally defective: Education, sterilization, euthanasia. *Journal of the American Psychiatry Association, 99,* 13–16.

Kennedy, R. G. (2003). *Mr. Jefferson's lost cause: Land, farmers, slavery, and the Louisiana Purchase.* Oxford: Oxford University Press.

Kitano, H. H. L., & Daniels, R. (2001). *Asian Americans: Emerging minorities* (3rd ed.). Upper Saddle River, NJ: Prentice Hall.

Kitchin, R. (1998). "Out of place," "knowing one's place": Space, power, and the exclusion of disabled people. *Disability and Society, 13,* 343–356.

Kitchin, R. (2000). The researched opinions on research: Disabled people and disability research. *Disability and Society, 15,* 25–47.

Kleck, R., Ono, H., & Hastorf, A. H. (1966). The effects of physical deviance upon face-to-face interaction. *Human Relations, 19*(4), 425–436.

Konkright, K. E. (2001). An analysis of the applicability of Title III of the Americans with Disabilities Act to private Internet access providers. *Idaho Law Review, 37,* 713–746.

Korematsu v. United States, 323 U.S. 214 (1944).

Kruse, D., & Hale, T. (2003). Disability and employment: Symposium introduction. *Industrial Relations, 42,* 1–10.

Kruse, D., & Schur, L. (2003). Employment of people with disabilities following the ADA. *Industrial Relations, 42,* 31–66.

Lacheen, C. (2000). Achy breaky pelvis, lumber lung and juggler's despair: The portrayal of the Americans with Disabilities Act on television and radio. *Berkeley Journal of Employment and Labor Law, 21,* 223–245.

Lais, S. (2000). Accessibility law evokes cheers, fears. *Computerworld, 34*(17), 97.

Lane v. Pena, 867 F. Supp. 1050 (D.D.C. 1994), *affirmed* 518 U.S. 187 (1996).

Lane, J. P. (2002). Are Web sites a "public accommodation" under Title III of the Americans with Disabilities Act ("ADA") requiring reasonable access for persons with disabilities? *Legal Reference Quarterly, 21,* 1–23.

Lang, H. G. (2000). *A phone of our own: The deaf insurrection against Ma Bell.* Washington, DC: Gallaudet University Press.

Larsen, E., & Rainie, L. (2002). *The rise of the e-citizen: How people use government agencies' Web sites.* Washington, DC: Pew Internet and American Life Project.

Lau Ow Bew v. U.S., 144 U.S. 47 (1892).

Lawrence, D. H. (2001). *Lady Chatterley's lover.* New York: Modern Library.

Lawrence, G. (1947). Some facts concerning sterilization based upon a study in Orange County, North Carolina. *North Carolina Medical Journal, 8,* 19–25.

Lazar, J., Beere, P., Greenridge, K., & Nagappa, Y. (2003). Web accessibility in the mid-Atlantic United States: A study of 50 homepages. *Universal Access in the Information Society, 2,* 331–341.

Lazar, J., Dudley-Sponaugle, A., & Greenidge, K.-D. (2004). Improving web accessibility: A study of webmaster perceptions. *Computers in Human Behavior, 20*, 269–288.

Lee, B. A. (2003). A decade of the Americans with Disabilities Act: Judical outcomes and unresolved problems. *Industrial Relations, 42*, 11–30.

Lee, H. (1997). *Virginia Woolf.* New York: A. A. Knopf.

Lesbian/Gay Freedom Day Committee, Inc. v. U.S. I.N.S., 541 F. Supp. 569 (N.D. Cal.), *affirmed* 714 U.S. 1470 (1982).

Leslie Harris & Associates. (2002). *Bringing a nation online: The importance of federal leadership.* Available: http://civilrights.org/publications/bringinganationonline.

Levine, G. (2002). *Dying to know: Scientific epistemology and narrative in Victorian England.* Chicago: University of Chicago Press.

Levitin, T. E. (1975). Deviants as active participants in the labeling process: The visibly handicapped. *Social Problems, 22*, 548–557.

Linton, S. (1998a). *Claiming disability: Knowledge and identity.* New York: New York University Press.

Linton, S. (1998b). Disability studies/not disability studies. *Disability and Society, 13*(4), 525–540.

Livneh, H. (1982). On the origins of negative attitudes toward people with disabilities. *Rehabilitation Literature, 43*, 338–347.

Loewen, J. W. (1995). *Lies my teacher told: Everything your American history textbook got wrong.* New York: Touchstone.

Longmore, P. (1987). Images of disabled people in television and motion pictures. In A. Garner & T. Joe (Eds.), *Images of the disabled, disabling images* (pp. 65–78). New York: Praeger.

Longmore, P. K. (2003). *Why I burned my book and other essays on disability.* Philadelphia: Temple University Press.

Longmore, P. K., & Umansky, L. (Eds.). (2001). *The new disability history: American perspectives.* New York: New York University Press.

Lonsdale, S. (1990). *Women and disability.* New York: Macmillan.

Looe Shee v. North, 170 F. 566 (9th Cir. 1909).

Lowe, R. (2000). Eugenics, scientific racism and education: Has anything changed over one hundred years? In M. Crotty, J. Germov, & G. Rodwell (Eds.), *"A race for a place": Eugenics, Darwinism, and social thought and practice in Australia* (pp. 207–220). Newcastle, AU: University of Newcastle Press.

Lyons, J. (1999). Mentally disabled citizenship applicants and the meaningful oath requirement for naturalization. *California Law Review, 87*, 1017–1049.

Mackenzie, D. A. (1981). *Statistics in Britain, 1865–1930.* Edinburgh: Edinburgh University Press.

Mairs, N. (1996). *Waist-high in the world: A life among the nondisabled.* Boston: Beacon Press.

Makas, E. (1988). Positive attitudes toward disabled people: Disabled and nondisabled persons' perspectives. *Journal of Social Issues, 44*(1), 49–61.

Mandel, C. A., & Wolven, R. (1996). Intellectual access to digital documents: Joining proven principles with new technologies. *Cataloging and Classification Quarterly, 22*(3/4), 25–42.

Marincu, C., & McMullin, B. (2004). A comparative analysis of Web accessibility and technical standards conformance in four EU states. *First Monday, 9*(7). Available: http://www.firstmonday.org/issues/issue9_7/marincu/index.html.

Marks, D. (1999). *Disability: Controversial debates and psychological perspectives.* New York: Routledge.

Maroney, P. (2000). The wrong tool for the right job: Are commercial websites places of public accommodation under the Americans with Disabilities Act of 1990? *Vanderbilt Journal of Entertainment Law and Practice, 2,* 191–204.

Mates, B. T. (1991). *Library technology for visually and physically impaired patrons.* Westport, CT: Meckler.

Matthews, W. (2001a, November 5). A legal tangle: Litigation worries over accessibility law spark agency/contractor disputes. *Federal Computer Week.* Available: http://www.fcw.com.

Matthews, W. (2001b, October 22). Web usability obstacles abound. *Federal Computer Week.* Available: http://www.fcw.com.

Matthews, W. (2002, June 24). One year and counting: Section 508—Feds tout progress but need more time on accessibility law. *Federal Computer Week.* Available: http://www.fcw.com.

McClesky, J., Henry, D., & Hodges, D. (1998). Inclusion: Where is it happening? *Teaching Exceptional Children, 31,* 4–10.

McClung, M. (1974). Do handicapped children have a legal right to a minimally adequate education? *Journal of Law and Education, 3,* 153–173.

McDonald, P. (1991, March 8). Double discrimination must be faced now. *Disability Now,* 7–8.

McGuire, J. F. (1994). Organizing from diversity in the name of community: Lessons from the disability civil rights movement. *Policy Studies Journal, 22*(1), 112–123.

McLawhorn, L. (2001). Leveling the accessibility playing field: Section 508 of the Rehabilitation Act. *North Carolina Journal of Law and Technology, 3,* 63–100.

McNulty, T. (Ed.). (1999). *Accessible libraries on campus: A practical guide for the creation of disability-friendly libraries.* Chicago: Association of College and Research Libraries.

McRuer, R. (2003). As good as it gets: Queer theory and critical disability. *GLQ: A Journal of Gay and Lesbian Studies, 9*(1-2), 79–105.

Melville, H. (1967). *Moby Dick.* New York: Norton. (Original work published 1851)

Menand, L. (2001). *The metaphysical club: A story of ideas in America.* New York: Farrar, Straus and Giroux.

Metts, R. L. (2000). *Disability issues, trends and recommendations for the World Bank.* Washington, DC: World Bank.

Michael, S. (2004, April 19). Making government accessible—online. *Federal Computer Week,* 24–30.

Milliman, R. E. (2002). Website accessibility and the private sector: Disability stakeholders cannot tolerate 2% access! *Information Technology and Disabilities, 8*(2). Available: http://www.rit.edu/~easi.itd.htm.

Mills v. Board of Education, 348 F. Supp. 866 (D. DC 1972).

Milton, J. (1936). On his blindness. In T. Newton (Ed.), *Complete poems* (pp. 613–614). Englewood Cliffs, NJ: Prentice-Hall.

Mondak, J. (1989). The politics of professional wrestling. *Journal of Popular Culture, 23,* 139–14.

Montaigne, M. (1958). Of a monstrous child. In D. M. Frame (Ed.), *Complete works* (pp. 538–539). Stanford, CA: Stanford University Press.

Morris, J. (1991). *Pride against prejudice: Transforming attitudes to disability.* London: Women's Press.

Morris, M. H. (1980). Gay rights: Can the courts light the way. *Los Angeles Lawyer, 3,* 18–24.

Morton, T. G. (1897). *The history of Pennsylvania Hospital 1751–1895.* Philadelphia: Times.

Mueller, J. P. (2003). *Accessibility for everybody: Understanding the Section 508 accessibility requirements.* New York: Springer-Verlag.

Muir, A., & Oppenheim, C. (2002a). National information policy developments worldwide I: Electronic government. *Journal of Information Science, 28*(3), 173–186.

Muir, A., & Oppenheim, C. (2002b). National information policy developments worldwide II: Universal access—addressing the digital divide. *Journal of Information Science, 28*(4), 263–273.

Murphy v. United Parcel Service, 527 U.S. 516 (1999).

Nadler, D. M., & Furman, V. M. (2001). Access board issues final standards for disabled access under Section 508 of Rehabilitation Act. *Government Contract Litigation Reporter, 14*(19), 14.

National Council on Disability. (2001). *The accessible future.* Available: http://www.ncd.gov.

National Council on Disability. (2002). *The Americans with Disabilities Act policy brief series: Righting the ADA—broad or narrow construction of the ADA.* Available: http://www.ncd.gov.

National Council on Disability. (2003a). *The Americans with Disabilities Act policy brief series: Righting the ADA—defining "disability" in a civil rights context: The court's focus on the extent of limitations as opposed to fair treatment and equal opportunity.* Available: http://www.ncd.gov.

National Council on Disability. (2003b). *The Americans with Disabilities Act policy brief series: Righting the ADA—the impact of the Supreme Court's ADA decisions on the rights of persons with disabilities.* Available: http://www.ncd.gov.

National Health Interview Survey. (2002). *Disability and religion.* Hyattsville, MD: National Center for Health Statistics.

National Information Center. (2000). *Benchmarking the e-government revolution: Year 2000 report on citizen and business demand.* Washington, DC: Author.

National Organization on Disability. (2003). *The religious participation gap.* Washington, DC: Author.

Nelson, J. (1996). The invisible cultural group: Images of disability. In P.M. Lester (Ed.), *Images that injure: Pictorial stereotypes in the media* (pp. 119–126). Westport, CT: Praeger.

Nelson, T. D. (Spring, 1997). Congressional attention needed for the stay-put provision of the Individuals with Disabilities Education Act. *Brigham Young University Education and Law Journal,* 49–68.

Neugebauer, R. G. (1996). Mental handicap in medieval and early modern England: Criteria measurement and care. In D. Wright & A. Digby (Eds.), *From idiocy to mental deficiency: Historical perspectives on people with learning disabilities* (pp. 22–43). New York: Routledge.

Neville, A., & Datray, T. (1993). Planning for equal intellectual access for blind and low vision users. *Library Hi Tech, 11*(1), 67–71.

Newcombe, T. (2001, December). Unequal access: Patchwork of policies creates uncertain e-government availability for citizens with disabilities. *Government Technology, 25.*

Noel v. Chapman, 508 F.2d 1023 (2nd Cir. 1975).

Noll, S. (1995). *Feeble-minded in our midst: Institutions for the mentally retarded in the south, 1900–1940.* Chapel Hill: University of North Carolina Press.

Norden, M. F. (1994). *The cinema of isolation: A history of physical difference in the movies.* New Brunswick, NJ: Rutgers University Press.

Norris, P. (2001). *Digital divide: Civic engagement, information poverty, and the Internet worldwide.* Cambridge: Cambridge University Press.

Oliver, M. (1990). *The politics of disablement.* London: Macmillan.

Oliver, M., & Barnes, C. (1998). *Disabled people and social policy: From exclusion to inclusion.* London: Longman.

Olkin, R., & Howson, L. J. (1994). Attitudes toward and images of physical disability. *Journal of Social Behavior and Personality, 9*(5), 81–96.

Opinion of the Attorney General 18, 500 (1886).

Opinion of the Attorney General 20, 79 (1891a).

Opinion of the Attorney General 22, 122 (1891b).

Opinion of the Attorney General 24, 706 (1903).

Park, J. S. W. (2004). *Elusive citizenship: Immigration, Asian Americans, and the paradox of civil rights.* New York: New York University Press.

Patterson, D. (2002). Along the disability divide. *Government Technology's Electronic Government, 3*(1), 8–13.

Pennsylvania Association for Retarded Children (PARC) v. Commonwealth of Pennsylvania, 334 F. Supp. 1257 (E.D.Pa. 1971).

People v. Caldwell, 603 N.Y.S.2d 713 (N. Y. App. Term, 1995).

Pernick, M. S. (1997). Defining the defective: Eugenics, aesthetics, mass culture in early-twentieth-century America. In D. T. Mitchell & S. L. Snyder (Eds.), *The body and physical difference: Discourses of disability* (pp. 89–110). Ann Arbor: University of Michigan Press.

Peterson, W. (1998). Public policy affecting universal design. *Assistive Technology, 10*(1), 13–20.

Petition of Rubenstein, 637 A.2d 1131 (Del. Supr. 1994).

Petruzzelli, J. D. (2001). Adjust your font size: Websites are public accommodations under the Americans with Disabilities Act. *Rutgers Law Review, 53,* 1063–1093.

Pfeiffer, D. (1993). Overview of the disability movement: History, legislative record, and political implications. *Policy Studies Journal, 21*(4), 724–735.

Pfeiffer, D. (1999). Eugenics and disability discrimination. In R. P. Marinelli & A. E. Dell Orto (Eds.), *The psychological and social impact of disability* (4th ed., pp. 12–31). New York: Springer.

Pfeiffer, D. (2000). The disability paradigm. *Journal of Disability Policy Studies, 11*(2), 98–99.

Pinker, S. (2002). *The blank slate: The modern denial of human nature*. New York: Viking.

Pitts, J., & Stripling, B. (1990, Spring). Information power challenge: To provide intellectual and physical access. *School Library Media Quarterly*, 133–134.

Pointon, A., & Davies, C. (1997). *Framed: Interrogating disability in the media*. London: British Film Institute.

Portes, A., & Rumbaut, R. G. (1996). *Immigrant America: A portrait* (2nd ed.). Berkeley: University of California Press.

Priestley, M. (2001). Introduction: The global context of disability. In M. Priestley (Ed.), *Disability and the life course: Global perspectives* (pp. 3–14). Cambridge: Cambridge University Press.

Proctor, R. N. (2002). Eugenics in Hitler's Germany. In D. F. Ryan & J. S. Schuchman (Eds.), *Deaf people in Hitler's Europe* (pp. 32–48). Washington, DC: Gallaudet University Press.

Puskin v. Regents of the University of Colorado, 658 F.2d 1372 (10th Cir. 1981).

Rachelson, A. D. (1997). Expelling students who claim to be disabled: Escaping the Individuals with Disabilities Education Act's "stay-put" provision. *Michigan Law and Policy Review, 2*, 127–158.

Ramsingh, O. M. (1995). Disciplining children with disabilities under the Individuals with Disabilities Education Act. *Journal of Contemporary Health Law and Policy, 12*, 155–181.

Ranen, J. S. (2002). Was blind but now I see: The argument for ADA applicability to the Internet. *Boston College Third World Law Journal, 22*, 389–418.

Rankin, V. (1992, March). Pre-search: Intellectual access to information. *School Library Journal*, 168–170.

Ransom, P. (1994). Public policy/legislative trends: Telecommunications access for people with disabilities. *Technology and Disability, 3*(3), 165–172.

Rapp, R., & Ginsburg, F. (2001). Enabling disability: Rewriting kinship, reimagining citizenship. *Public Culture, 13*(3), 533–556.

Rebell, M. (1986). Structural discrimination and the rights of the disabled. *Georgetown Law Journal, 74*, 1435–1489.

Rehabilitation Act, 29 U.S.C.A. § 701 *et seq.* (1973).

Rehabilitation Act regulations, 34 C.F.R. § 104 *et seq.*

Reilly, P. R. (1991). *The surgical solution: A history of involuntary sterilization in the United States*. Baltimore: Johns Hopkins University Press.

Reinders, H. S. (2000). *The future of the disabled in liberal society: An ethical analysis*. Notre Dame, IN: University of Notre Dame Press.

Rendon v. Valley Crest Productions, D. C. Docket No. 00-00830-CV-FAM, 11th Cir. (June 18, 2002).

Rich, R. F., Erb, C. T., & Rich, R. A. (2002). Critical legal and policy issues for people with disabilities. *DePaul Journal of Health Care Law, 6*, 1–53.

Richards, R. J. (1987). *Darwin and the emergence of evolutionary theories of mind and behavior*. Chicago: University of Chicago Press.

Richardson, S. A. (1963). Some social psychological consequences of handicapping. *Pediatrics, 32*, 291–297.

Riddell, S. (1996). Theorising special education needs in a changing political climate. In L. Barton (Ed.), *Disability and society: Emerging issues and insights* (pp. 83–106). London: Addison Wesley Longman.

Ridley, M. (1999). *Genome: The autobiography of a species in 23 chapters*. New York: HarperCollins.

Rioux, M. H. (1994). Towards a concept of equality of well-being: Overcoming the social and legal construction of inequality. In M. H. Rioux & M. Bach (Eds.), *Disability is not measles* (pp. 67–108). North York, Ontario: Roeher Institute.

Robertson, C. B. (2001). Providing access to the future: How the Americans with Disabilities Act can remove barriers in cyberspace. *Denver University Law Review, 79*, 199–227.

Rosen, G. (1968). *Madness in society: Chapters in the historical sociology of mental illness*. Chicago: University of Chicago Press.

Rosenberg v. Fleutti, 374 U.S. 449 (1963).

Rushton, P. (1996). Idiocy, the family and community in early modern northeast England. In D. Wright & A. Digby (Eds.), *From idiocy to mental deficiency: Historical perspectives on people with learning disabilities* (pp. 44–64). New York: Routledge.

Salder, J. E. (1966). *J. A. Comenius and the concept of universal education*. New York: Barnes and Noble.

Samuels, E. J. (2003). My body, my closet: Invisible disability and the limits of coming-out discourse. *GLQ: A Journal of Gay and Lesbian Studies, 9*(1–2), 233–255.

Samure, K., & Given, L. M. (2004). Digitally enhanced? An examination of the information behaviors of visually impaired post-secondary students. *Canadian Journal of Information and Library Science, 28*(2), 25–42.

Saunders v. Horn, 959 F. Supp. 689 (E.D.Pa. 1996).

Schartz, K., Schartz, H. A., & Blanck, P. (2002). Employment of persons with disabilities in information technology jobs: Literature review for "IT Works." *Behavioral Sciences and the Law, 20*, 637–657.

Scheer, J., & Groce, N. (1988). Impairment as human constant: Cross-cultural and historical perspectives on variation. *Journal of Social Issues, 44*(1), 23–37.

Schloss, A. M. (2001). Web-sight for visually-disabled people: Does Title III of the Americans with Disabilities Act apply to Internet Websites? *Columbia Journal of Law and Social Problems, 35*, 35–59.

Schmetzke, A. (2002). Accessibility of Web-based information resources for people with disabilities. *Library Hi Tech, 20*(2), 135–136.

Schneider, C. R., & Anderson, W. (1980). Attitudes toward the stigmatized: Some insights into recent research. *Rehabilitation Counseling Bulletin, 23*, 299–313.

Schur, L. A. (2003a). Barriers or opportunities? The causes of contingent and part-time work among people with disabilities. *Industrial Relations, 42*, 589–622.

Schur, L. A. (2003b). Contending with the "double handicap": Political activism among women with disabilities. *Women and Politics, 25*(1/2), 31–62.

Scotch, R. K. (2001). *From goodwill to civil rights: Transforming federal disability policy* (2nd ed.). Philadelphia: Temple University Press.

Scotch, R. K., & Schriner, K. (1997). Disability as human variation: Implications for policy. *Annals of the American Academy of Political and Social Science, 549*, 148–159.

Section 508 of the Rehabilitation Act, 29 U.S.C. § 794d. (1998).

Seguin, E. (1846). *The moral treatment, hygiene, and education of idiots and other backward children*. Paris: Bailliere.

Shakespeare, T. S. (1994). Cultural representations of disabled people: Dustbins for disavowal. *Disability and Society, 9*(3), 283–301.

Shapiro, J. P. (1993). *No pity: People with disabilities forging a new civil rights movement.* New York: Times Books.

Shapiro, J. P. (1994). Disability policy and the media: A stealth civil rights movement bypasses the press and defies conventional wisdom. *Policy Studies Journal, 22,* 123–133.

Shorter, E. (2000). *The Kennedy family and the story of mental retardation.* Philadelphia: Temple University Press.

Siebers, T. (2001). Disability in theory: From social constructionism to the new realism of the body. *American Literary History, 13*(4), 737–745.

Siebers, T. (2003). What can disability studies learn from the culture wars? *Cultural Critique, 55,* 182–216.

Silvers, A. (1998). Formal justice. In A. Silvers, D. Wasserman, & M. Mahowald (Eds.), *Disability, difference, and discrimination* (pp. 13–145). Lanham, MD: Rowman and Littlefield.

Silvers, A. (2000). The unprotected: Constructing disability in the context of anti-discrimination law. In L. P. Francis & A. Silvers (Eds.), *Americans with disabilities: Exploring implications of the law for individuals with disabilities* (pp. 126–145). New York: Routledge.

Slatin, J. M., & Rush, S. (2003). *Maximum accessibility.* Boston: Addison Wesley.

Smith, D. D. (2001). Special education: Teaching in an age of opportunity. Boston: Allyn and Bacon.

Smith, S., Wilkinson, M. W., & Wagoner, L. C. (1914). *A summary of the laws of the several states governing marriage and divorce of the feebleminded, epileptic and the insane; asexualization; and institutional commitment and discharge of the feebleminded and the epileptic.* Seattle: University of Washington.

Sparks, C. (1993). Raymond Williams and the theory of democratic communication. In S. Splichal & J. Wasko (Eds.), *Communication and democracy* (pp. 69–86). Norwood, NJ: Ablex.

Spring, J. (1993). *Conflict of interests: The politics of American education* (2nd ed.). New York: Longman.

Stanton, J. F. (1996). The immigration laws from a disability perspective: Where we were, where we are, where we should be. *Georgetown Immigration Law Journal, 10,* 441–465.

Stephanidis, C., & Savidis, A. (2001). Universal access in the information society: Methods, tools, and interactive technologies. *Universal Access in the Information Society, 1,* 40–55.

Stewart, T. G. (2000). Government, politics, and disability policy. *Journal of Disability Policy Studies, 11*(2), 109–110.

Stick, R. S. (1976). The handicapped child has a right to an appropriate education. *Nebraska Law Review, 55,* 637–682.

Stiker, H. J. (1999). *A history of disability* (W. Sayers, Trans.). Ann Arbor: University of Michigan Press.

Stokes, W. E. D. (1917). *The right to be well born or horse breeding in its relation to eugenics.* New York: C. J. O'Brien.

Stone, D. A. (1984). *The disabled state.* London: Macmillan.

Stone, E. (1999). Modern slogan, ancient script: Impairment and disability in the Chinese language. In M. Corker & S. French (Eds.), *Disability discourse* (pp. 136–147). Philadelphia: Open University Press.

Stone, E., & Priestly, M. (1996). Parasites, prawns and partners: Disability research and the role of non-disabled researchers. *British Journal of Sociology, 47*, 699–716.

Stowers, G. N. L. (2002). *The state of federal Websites: The pursuit of excellence.* Available: http://www.endowment.pwcglobal.com/pdfs/StowersReport0802.pdf.

Stuart, O. (1992). Race and disability: Just a double oppression? *Disability, Handicap and Society, 7*(2), 177–188.

A survey of government and the Internet: The next revolution. (2000, June 24). *The Economist, 2.*

Sutton v. United Air Lines, Inc., 527 U.S. 471 (1999).

Svenonius, E. (2000). *The intellectual foundation of information organization.* Cambridge, MA: MIT Press.

Swain, J., French, S., & Cameron, C. (2003). *Controversial issues in a disabling society.* Philadelphia: Open University Press.

Switzer, J. V. (2003). *Disabled rights: American disability policy and the fight for equality.* Washington, DC: Georgetown University Press.

Tang, B. A. (2001). Section 508 tips from the trenches. *Federal Computer Week.* Available: http://www.fcw.com.

Taylor, P. (2001). The Americans with Disabilities Act and the Internet. *Boston University Journal of Science and Technology Law, 7*, 26–51.

Telecommunications Act of 1996, 47 U.S.C.A. § 225 (1996).

Television Decoder Circuitry Act, P. L. No. 101–431, 104 Stat. 960 (1990).

Tennessee v. Lane, 2004 U.S. Lexis 3386 (2004).

Thibodeau, P. (2001). Fed access law could affect IT. *Computerworld, 35*(25), 1, 61.

Thomas, C. (1999). *Female forms: Experiencing and understanding disability.* Buckingham: Open University Press.

Thomas, D. (1982). *The experience of handicap.* London: Methuen.

Thomson, R. G. (1997). *Extraordinary bodies: Figuring disability in American culture and literature.* New York: Columbia University Press.

Tomasevsci, K. (1999). From healthism to social well-being: Health-related human rights of people with disabilities. In M. Jones & L. A. B. Marks (Eds.), *Disability, divers-ability, and legal change* (pp. 251–266). Boston: Martinus Nijhoff.

Toregas, C. (2001). The politics of e-gov: The upcoming struggle for redefining civic engagement. *National Civic Review, 90*(3), 235–240.

Toyota v. Williams, 534 U.S. 184 (2002).

Trible v. Gordon, 430 U.S. 762 (1977).

Tringo, J. L. (1970). The hierarchy of preference toward disability groups. *The Journal of Special Education, 4*(3), 295–307.

Tsai, S. S. H. (1983). *China and the overseas Chinese in the United States 1868–1911.* Fayetteville: University of Arkansas Press.

Tucker, B. P. (2000). The Supreme Court's definition of disability under the ADA: A return to the dark ages. *Alabama Law Review, 52*, 321–374.

Tullman v. Tod, 294 F. 87 (2nd Cir. 1923).

Turnbull, H. R., Jr., & Stowe, M. J. (2001). Five models for thinking about disability: Implications for policy responses. *Journal of Disability Policy Studies, 12*(3), 198–205.

Turnbull, H. R., Jr., Wilcox, B. L., Stowe, M. J., & Umbarger, G. T., III (2001). Matrix of federal statutes and federal and state court decisions reflecting the core concepts of disability policy. *Journal of Disability Policy Studies, 12*(3), 144–176.

United Nations. (1982). *World Programme of Action Concerning Disabled Persons.* New York: Author.

United Nations. (1994). *Standard Rules on the Equalization of Opportunities for Persons with Disabilities.* New York: Author.

United States Commission on Civil Rights. (1997). *Equal educational opportunity and nondiscrimination for students with disabilities: Federal enforcement of Section 504.* Washington, DC: Author.

United States ex rel. Mandel v. Day, 19 F.2d 520 (D.C.N.Y. 1927).

United States ex rel. Markin v. Curran, 9 F.2d 900 (N.Y.), *cert. denied,* 270 U.S. 647 (1925).

United States ex rel. Patton v. Tod, 297 F. 385 (N.Y. 1924).

United States ex rel. Saclarides v. Shaughnessy, 180 F.2d 687 (N.Y. 1950).

United States ex. rel. Wulf v. Esperdy, 277 F.2d 537 (2nd Cir.1960).

United States v. Gue Lim, 176 U.S. 459 (1899).

United States v. Schwarz, 82 F.Supp. 933 (S.D.N.Y. 1949).

United States v. Tod, 294 U.S. 820 (N.Y. 1923).

Vanderwood, M., McGrew, K. S., & Ysseldyke, J. E. (1998). Why we can't say much about students with disabilities during education reform. *Exceptional Children, 64,* 359–370.

Vash, C. L., & Crewe, N. M. (2004). *Psychology of disability.* New York: Springer.

Vinen, R. (2000). *A history in fragments: Europe in the twentieth century.* New York: De Capo.

Wahl, O. (1995). *Media madness: Public images of mental illness.* New Brunswick, NJ: Rutgers University Press.

Ware, L. P. (2002). A moral conversation on disability: Risking the personal in educational contexts. *Hypatia, 17*(3), 143–172.

Warkany, J. (1959). Congenital malformations in the past. *Journal of Chronic Disabilities, 10,* 84–96.

Watson, A. (Ed.). (1998). *The digest of Justinian* (2 vols.). Philadelphia: University of Pennsylvania Press.

Wattenberg, T. (2004). Beyond legal compliance: Communities of advocacy that support accessible online learning. *Internet and Higher Education, 7,* 123–139.

Wells, S. J. (2001). Is the ADA working? *HR Magazine, 46*(4), 38–46.

West, D. M. (2002a). *State and federal e-government in the United States.* Available: http://www.insidepolitics.org/egovt02us.html.

West, D. M. (2002b). *Urban e-government, 2002.* Available: http://www.insidepolitics.org/egovt02city.html.

West, D. M. (2003). *Achieving E-government for all: Highlights from a national survey.* Benton Foundation/Rockefeller Institute of Government. Available: http://www.benton.org/publibrary/egov/access2003.doc.

West, T. G. (1997). *Vindicating the founders: Race, sex, class, and justice in the origins of America.* New York: Rowman and Littlefield.

Westbrook, M. T., Legge, V., & Pennay, M. (1993). Attitudes towards disabilities in a multicultural society. *Social Science and Medicine, 36,* 615–623.

Willeford, W. (1969). *The fool and his sceptre: A study in clowns and jesters and their audience.* London: Edward Arnold.

Williams, R. (1963). *Culture and society: 1780–1950.* New York: Harper and Row.

Williams, T. (2001). Making government services accessible. *American City and County, 116*(2), 12.

Wilson, W. (1902). *The history of the American people.* New York: Harper and Brothers.

Winship, M. P. (1994). Prodigies, Puritanism, and the perils of natural philosophy: The example of Cotton Mather. *The William and Mary Quarterly, 51,* 92–105.

Winzer, M. A. (1993). *The history of special education: From isolation to integration.* Washington, DC: Gallaudet University Press.

Winzer, M. A. (1997). Disability and society before the eighteenth century: Dread and despair. In L. J. Davis (Ed.), *The disability studies reader* (pp. 75–109). New York: Routledge.

Wolbring, G. (2003). Disability rights approach to bioethics? *Journal of Disability Policy Studies, 14*(3), 174–180.

Wolfsenberger, W. (1969). The origin and nature of our institutional models. In R. B. Kugel & W. Wolfsenberger (Eds.), *Changing patterns in residential services for the mentally retarded* (pp. 59–171). Washington, DC: President's Commission on Metal Retardation.

World Markets Research Centre. (2001). *Global e-government survey.* Providence, RI: Author.

World Wide Web Consortium. (1998). *Web content accessibility guidelines.* Available at http://www.w3c.org.

Wright, K. C., & Davie, J. F. (1991). *Serving the disabled: A how-to-do-it manual for librarians.* New York: Neal-Schumann.

Yans-McLaughlin, V. (1990). Introduction. In V. Yans-McLaughlin (Ed.), *Immigration reconsidered: History, sociology, and politics* (pp. 3–18). New York: Oxford University Press.

Yelin, E .H. (1992). *Disability and the displaced worker.* New Brunswick, NJ: Rutgers University Press.

Yu, P. K. (2002). Bridging the digital divide: Equality in the information age. *Cardozo Art and Entertainment Law Journal, 20,* 1–52.

Zahn, M. A. (1973). Incapacity, impotence, and invisible impairment: Their effects on interpersonal relations. *Journal of Health and Social Behavior, 14,* 115–123.

Ziporyn, T. (1992). *Nameless diseases.* New Brunswick, NJ: Rutgers University Press.

Zola, I. K. (1993). Disability statistics, what we count and what it tells us: A personal and political analysis. *Journal of Disability Policy Studies, 4*(2), 9–39.

Zola, I. K. (1994). Towards inclusion: The role of people with disabilities in policy and research issues in the United States—a historical and political analysis. In M. H. Rioux & M. Bach (Eds.), *Disability is not measles: New research paradigms in disability* (pp. 49–66). North York, Ontario: Roeher Institute.

Index

A *Beautiful Mind*, 106
Abortion, 36–37, 124–26
Access, 5, 9, 13, 26, 30, 39, 41–42, 44,
  59, 63–73, 75–83, 85–92, 121–24,
  128, 133–34, 136–37; intellectual
  access, 63, 67–73, 79–83, 123–24;
  physical access, 63–67, 69–73,
  79–83, 123–24
Access Board, 80
Access routes, 65–66
Accessible technologies, 41–42, 69–73,
  82–83, 85–92, 121, 123–24
Accessibility. *See* Accessible
  technologies
Advertising, 100–101, 106
Africa, 56
Air Carrier Access Act, 76
American Revolution, 30–32
Americans with Disabilities Act (ADA),
  41–45, 76–78, 81–83, 88, 126–28,
  132
Anxiety, 18, 21; aesthetic anxiety, 21;
  existential anxiety, 21
Architectural Barriers Act,
  79–80, 83
Asexualization. *See* Sterilization

Asia, 26, 51, 56–57
Assistive technologies, 26, 63–64, 67,
  70–72, 85
Australia, 13, 35, 46, 75–76,
  79, 136
Austria, 46, 75–76
Autobiography of a Face (Grealy),
  108–9

Bacon, Francis, 105
Baker, Hilda, 112
*Beggars Who Get About on Their Own in
  Bordeaux* (de Goya), 114
Begging, 4, 26, 29, 45, 114–15
Bell, Alexander Graham, 33
Bitter Strength, 51
Black Panthers, 41
Black Stork, The, 36
Bond, Thomas, 30
Born on the Fourth of July, 106
Bourne, Randolph, 39
Brazil, 27, 46, 75–76
Britain. *See* United Kingdom
Brown, Christy, 98
Burton, Phillip, 41
Bush, George H. W., 41

About the Authors

PAUL T. JAEGER is Manager for Research Development at the Information Use Management and Policy Institute of the School of Information Studies at Florida State University and is a doctoral candidate at Florida State University's College of Information. He has earned a Juris Doctor with Honors and master's degrees in information studies and education. His publications have addressed issues of disability and accessibility, information access, education, constitutional law, electronic government, and information policy and law.

CYNTHIA ANN BOWMAN is Associate Professor of Literacy Education at Ashland University. She received her PhD in 1996 from Kent State University in Curriculum and Instruction with an emphasis in English Education. A former high school English teacher in Daytona Beach, Florida, Cindy has also taught at Ball State University and Florida State University. Currently she serves on the Teacher Advisory Group of PBS. President of the Ohio Council of Teachers of English Language Arts, she is also active in the National Council of Teachers of English, the International Reading Association, the American Educational Research Association, and the Society for Information Technology and Teacher Education.

CPSIA information can be obtained
at www.ICGtesting.com
Printed in the USA
FSOW04n0317270617
35619FS